THE RAISING OF THE VASA

THE RAISING
OF
THE VASA

The rebirth of a Swedish galleon

ROY SAUNDERS

OLDBOURNE
LONDON

OLDBOURNE BOOK CO. LTD.
121 Fleet Street, London E.C.4

Printed and bound in Great Britain
by Purnell and Sons, Ltd. Paulton (Somerset) and London

To my wife and son

IRENE and GARETH

who shared with me the pilgrimage to Stockholm

to see the mighty Vasa

"They mark our passage as a race of men,

Earth shall not see such ships as these again . . ."

ACKNOWLEDGEMENTS

AMONG many who helped in the preparation of this book, I would like to acknowledge a special debt of gratitude to:

Anders Franzén, discoverer of the *Vasa*.
Dr. Erik Lars Barkman, Chief Chemical Engineer at the Preservation Centre.
Thure Lagerstrom, Flygt Pumps.
Philip Lorrain, Sydney Barton Ltd., Stockholm.
Anthony Paul Baird, Swedish Radio.
Lars Widding, *Expressen*.
Commodore Edward Clason.
Lars Arno, Royal Ministry of Foreign Affairs, Stockholm.
Goran Landberg, Press Attaché, Swedish Embassy, London.
Nils Sallstedt, Official Photographer to Vasanämnden.
Captain Axel Hedberg, Chief Salvage Officer, Neptun Company.
Bengt Hallvards, P.R.O. Vasanämnden.
John Weston Thomas, National Museum of Wales, Cardiff.
Norman Bisby, Cottingham, Yorkshire.
F. L. Hall, Industrial Pumps, Nottingham.
Burton C. Lemmon, Tacoma, U.S.A.

CONTENTS

9

SPECIFICATIONS OF THE *VASA*

Length :   162 feet.

Beam :   39 feet.

Displacement : 1,300 tons.

Armament :   64 guns, carried on three decks, including 48 twenty-four pounders.

Rigging :   It seems that she had three masts, and it is likely that the fore- and main-masts were square-rigged and that the mizzen-mast was square-rigged with a lateen sail.

LIST OF ILLUSTRATIONS

INTRODUCTION

IN all seafaring nations the names of certain ships and the stories that surround them, whether in fact or fiction, have been woven into the national literature. Britain has such names as *Mayflower*, *Bounty*, *Victory*, *Cutty Sark*, *Golden Hind*, and many others. Norway has its *Fram*, *Kon-Tiki*, and Oseberg Viking ship, among others, which have played their parts in exploration, trade, naval action or legend. Most of these ships have been lost and their graves are not known; others have been preserved for exhibition. But, whether lost or preserved, their stories have passed along the centuries to endure as long as sagas of the sea remain.

From the seventeenth-century empire of Sweden fragments of the story of a mighty galleon, *Vasa*, that sank within half a mile of the start of her maiden voyage, began one of the strangest of them all. Only traces of the story had been handed down to puzzle and tantalise historians and marine archaeologists who lived and worked within sight of her forgotten grave in the inner harbour of Stockholm—until her discovery in 1956 by Anders Franzén.

In the wonderful archipelago beyond Stockholm harbour, where the isles of Sweden make uneasy union between land and sea, lies the fabled cemetery of many ships of the ancient Baltic galleon fleet, their woodwork still strangely well preserved. For many years this

13

tideless sea was the hunting ground of Anders Franzén and his search for seventeenth-century wooden ships. He had already discovered the resting-places of several galleons that have still to reveal their secrets and treasures to those who have the means to raise them. During his quest Anders Franzén made an important discovery, that *Teredo navalis*, the "death-watch beetle" of the ocean, does not exist in the brackish waters of the Baltic; consequently, sunken ships have remained preserved, their timbers almost as sound after the passing of centuries as on the day of their sinking.

One of these ships, the *Vasa*, royal flagship of the great imperial fleet, sank near the entrance to the naval dockyard at the start of her maiden voyage in 1628. This book tells of Franzén's discovery of the ship and how the resources of his great city were applied to raise, after a three-year period of modern salvage work, the blackened wooden hull of the *Vasa*.

The lifting, excavation and preservation of this galleon has already cost over a million pounds, but has led to as great an unwrapping of history as many major discoveries of the century. The *Vasa* is nearly two hundred years older than Nelson's flagship *Victory*, preserved at Portsmouth, and it is rightly acclaimed the oldest fully identified ship in the world.

Now this great wooden weapon of the seventeenth century stands housed on public exhibition as she passes through stages of slow, careful preservation for posterity. The royal *Vasa* has already become a national monument, and eventually will take a rightful place among the wonders of the world.

CHAPTER I

As It Was

O N the afternoon of 10th August 1628 the city of
Stockholm was in a state of ferment. The great
church was crowded; citizens who lived in the surrounding districts had ridden in for the day as news spread
that in the evening, after vespers, the mighty battle
galleon *Vasa* was to sail on her maiden voyage to the
war in Europe. Sweden was fast becoming an important
military power under King Gustavus II Adolphus, the
"Northern Hurricane".

The emergence of this great Swedish king on the
European scene has been called a glorious epic in the
history of Sweden. It came at a time when Roman
Catholic persecution was driving the Protestant states
into arms, and quiet peasants were being converted
into fiery swordsmen. After the savagery of the Spanish
Catholic influence, Protestantism increased in dominance
in many countries. Thus the stage was set for the emergence of a leader on the grand scale, and the politico-
military epic of the Swedish king—the "Northern
Hurricane"—burst as a bulwark of the Protestant faith.

As the long succession of Gustavus Adolphus's victorious
battles took him ever deeper into Germany towards the
Austrian frontier, his lengthening lines of communication
brought the inevitable demand for bigger and better

ships. In 1625 the order was issued for the building of four new ships of war. These were intended to command the sea lanes of the Baltic between Stockholm and the Polish coast. The contract for building one of the ships—the *Vasa*—was signed on 10th January 1625.

She was to be greater than any warship previously built, and was the secret weapon of the day; her triple gun decks mounted sixty-four bronze cannon. She was planned for a leading role in the military achievements yet to come.

Hundreds of Stockholm families had contributed directly or indirectly to the *Vasa's* construction. In little more than two years shipwrights, carpenters, designers, sawyers, artists, wood-carvers, armourers, and blacksmiths had worked with apprentices and press-ganged labourers to build her. Great teams of horses carted carefully chosen baulks of oak, ash, lime, spruce, pine, linden and other woods from the forests. The construction of one wooden warship took forty acres of timber.

The overall dimensions of such fighting ships were usually laid down by authorised officers appointed by the king. In the case of the *Vasa* the king himself had dictated the measurements, and who in Europe would have dared to argue with him? Henrik Hybertsson, the designer, had built to Gustavus Adolphus's instructions probably against his better professional judgment. As the mighty weapon took shape Hybertsson may have foreseen the coming disaster, which by then he was powerless to avert. Before the *Vasa* was launched Henrik Hybertsson died, but the manner of his death is unrecorded.

Anders Franzén, discoverer of the Vasa, searching among the old archives for any clue that would help him to locate the sunken galleon.

The tool that found the Vasa. *Anders Franzén's core sampler which he used to search the harbour bed and with which he finally located the galleon.*

Frogmen photographers preparing to film details of the Vasa under water. The turbid condition of the harbour water rendered an ordinary underwater camera quite useless, consequently a glass box of clear water was mounted in front of the camera lens, and detailed pictures were made by filming through it.

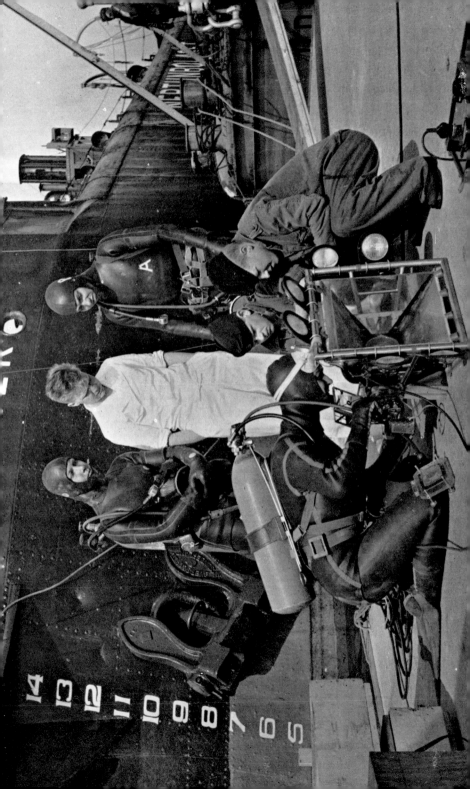

Demonstration by a diver of how he bored beneath the ship with the Zetterstrom-jet held before him.

As a warship the *Vasa* specifications included the requirements to sail swiftly; for her lower gun deck to ride clear of the water; to hold her sails firmly; steer well in action, and withstand the buffeting of the roughest seas.

The first specifications had decided her length and number of cannon, with room between the gun-ports for crews to load and fire with speed. As all ships are longer above than below, it had been necessary to determine her height, then her breadth of beam amidships, the depth of hold, the length of keel and angle of rake.

The width of each deck above water was reduced gradually to centralise the weight and minimise top-heaviness. But sufficient width had to be retained to allow for the recoil thrust of the cannon, the great weight of which was all above water level.

This must have been the scene as the great warship took shape. Apprentices and unskilled labourers worked on the more straightforward parts along the sides. The more experienced craftsmen steamed and fixed the curved timbers of the bow. The most highly skilled workers fashioned the complex curves and difficult construction of the stern. From early morning until late at night ceaseless hammering rang out from the Royal Dockyard, combined with the "chink" of the caulking-irons, the rasping from the saw-pits and the dull blows of the adzes. Over everything hung the sickly smell of fresh unseasoned wood, resinous pitch and Stockholm tar. Week after week the steaming and straining of the timbers continued, and gradually the massive oaken frames took on the shape of a giant ship at the head of the slipways. Slowly the close-set ribs were clad

with heavy timber walls, first on the outside, then on the inside of the ribs, until at last the hull was complete and ready for launching, a complex masterpiece of triple-laminated oaken walls eighteen inches thick. Then the giant web of masts and spars slowly rose above the city buildings until the topgallant on the mainmast of the *Vasa* soared to 190 feet above the naked hull and surrounding house-tops.

Then the carvings were brought from the workshops and assembled on the bow and round the high stern castle, and the *Vasa*, glowing with a fantastic adornment of colour and symbolism, became a thing of vivid baroque splendour. She was at the same time a weapon of war and a floating work of art. Everyone had worked longer hours to carry out the king's commands; disobedience incurred the death penalty, for Gustavus was closely following the ship's progress. Sweden in the early sixteen hundreds was well blessed in the raw materials for war; she had not only the man of the hour in Gustavus, but also the great copper mountain Stora Kopparberg, at Falun in central Sweden, where lay the richest deposits of copper ore in the western world. It was the possession of this mountain of copper that enabled Sweden to finance the wars which built up her empire to include Norway, Germany, Poland, Finland and parts of Russia. Copper coinage was introduced. Enormous rectangular coins were minted measuring thirty inches by twelve inches; they had great purchasing power but weighed forty pounds. Copper was the raw material for the making of bronze cannon, the "atomic weapon" of the seventeenth century. Gustavus was probably the only man in the world at

that date who could command (as he did) the immediate
building of four ships to be equipped with two hundred
and fifty-six new bronze cannon.

Orders had been despatched to Stora Kopparbergs
Bergslags Aktiebolag at Falun, which in 1625 was
already an ancient mining corporation whose records
as a shareholding company (probably the first in the
world) went back to June 1288. The king demanded
copper in enormous quantity, and the miners of Falun
went feverishly to work in the four-century-old crater
of the copper mountain. The rock face was heated
with wood fires, and the cracked ore-bearing rock
broken loose with crowbars; then it was crushed, roasted
and given a first smelting. Then it was re-roasted, and
finally smelted again into raw copper. The roasting
was done in fire pits, and the smelting in smelting huts
equipped with shaft furnaces heated by charcoal oxy-
genated by water-powered bellows.

An English traveller during the seventeenth century
visited Falun and records:

"When the wind is from the west, this smoke darkens
the city so that there is twilight at midday, and the in-
habitants must light torches to be able to go about
their business. All the private and public buildings in
the city are blackened by soot, and all the brass ornaments out of doors are covered by copper dust."

In the year 1650 three thousand and sixty-seven tons
of copper were produced from this one great pit. It is
not surprising that Queen Christina, Gustavus's daugh-
ter, said, "The greatness of the realm stands or falls
with the copper mountain."

The copper was delivered to the foundries and the

cannons were cast on time. They were heavily rein-
forced at the breech and beautifully moulded, chase-
girdled, with sturdy projecting trunnions on which to
balance on their carriages. At the breech end a cascabel
was cast to assist in the handling when taking aim, and
also to facilitate lashing down with heavy tackles when
the seas ran high. Each cannon bore the four moulded
letters G.A.R.S.—Gustavus Adolphus Rex Suecia.

The sixty-four cannons in position on *Vasa* weighed
nearly a hundred tons. The ship's ballast consisted of
one hundred and twenty tons of stone. The weight of
cannon balls, gunpowder and ancillary firearms is not
known. She was provisioned with some two thousand
one hundred casks of food, containing bread, herring,
dried fish, salted meat, pork, meal, peas, butter, grain,
salted eel, salmon and ale. She carried a crew of one
hundred and thirty-three sailors and a further complement of some three hundred men at arms. The *Vasa*
had a displacement of fourteen hundred tons.

As the afternoon of 10th August 1628 slipped into
early evening the excitement of the ever-growing crowd
that thronged the Skeppsbron between the palace and
the quayside steadily mounted.

The houses and buildings of the nobles and merchant
princes that looked down on the scene showed a similar
wealth of carving in stone to the carving in wood that
decorated the ship. The power of the Swedish empire
was in the ascendant, and this was reflected everywhere
in the stone sculpture that was lavished on the houses
of the rich.

As the great bell in the cathedral tolled the hour of
five *Vasa* was ready to sail. The ropes were cast off and

she was warped away from the shelter of the buildings against a gentle breeze from the south-west. Attendant boats rowed the ship's anchor to the full length of its cable and then released it, after which the capstan crew on the *Vasa* slowly wound in until the ship was drawn up to the anchor. The anchor would then be lifted and taken forward again by the boats. This would be repeated many times, as the mighty vessel slowly passed along the Skeppsbron quay, her ornate after-castle towering above the ranks of moored ketches, schooners, merchantmen and other sailing vessels that lined her path.

When she reached the neighbourhood of the cliffs of Sodermalm the anchor was drawn up and stowed. The fore topsail was set, then the main topsail, foresail and mizzen unfurled in the evening sunlight.

The crowd that thronged the Skeppsbron and the surrounding hills and islands would take personal pride and satisfaction in the sight of clean sheets of canvas taking the breeze as this creation of beauty which they had made began to move under the pressure of her filling sails. They had laboured for nearly three years; with the unflagging dedication of the Gothic stone carvers of an earlier age, they had produced a work of art more richly carved and ornamented than any ship that had preceded her. The stern parts were a riot of carved gods, demons, knights, kings, warriors, mermaids, cherubs and weird zoomorphic animal shapes ablaze with red and gold and blue. The symbols of courage, power, superstition and cruelty were portrayed to stir the imaginations of the superstitious sailors of the day.

As this floating gallery of so much creative art sailed away from the men who made it, a sense of emptiness must have lingered in many hearts, and tears of emotion must have sprung to many a watching eye.

The cannons of all the warships in the harbour thundered a farewell salute, to which the giant *Vasa* proudly fired her reply. As she emerged from her gun-smoke with flags flying, pennants waving, and gently filling sails, the brilliant colour of her superstructure ablaze and the water foaming about her rounded bow, she presented a more majestic spectacle than Stockholmers could have ever seen. Rows of gun-ports from which the cannons had fired were open, and from them peeped bronze muzzles, glinting in the sun. On every gun-port cover the carved mask of the Vasa lion glared in red and gold.

Then, according to the contemporary report, the wind freshened, there came a sudden squall and the ship listed heavily to port. There was consternation among the passengers. The sails were being tended, but there was not sufficient wind to pull them through the blocks.

The chief ordnance officer, Erik Jonsson, ran below to order the port-side cannon to be heaved over to starboard to counteract the list. The steepening angle of the gun decks increased alarmingly and he was too late. A sound like thunder reached the watchers on the shore as the cargo, ballast, ammunition and the four hundred people on board went crashing to the port side of the steeply listing ship. The lower gun-ports sank below water level, and an inrush of water sealed the *Vasa's* fate. In a few moments it was all over: the ship that was intended to rule the Baltic Sea sank into

the water with all flags flying. The mighty *Vasa* had foundered in the harbour of her birth.

The number of people drowned in the disaster has not been recorded, but the Danish captain, Severin Hansson, was among the rescued. He was immediately put in jail and closely questioned. He testified that all the cannon were lashed and that everyone was sober.

Two days later the Council of Ministers sent a despatch to the king informing him of the tragic news. In the following month a naval court of enquiry investigated the evidence of people most intimately concerned with the ship's construction, but no guilt or negligence was established, and no one was punished. Henrik Hybertsson had died in the previous year, and as the king had dictated the dimensions of the ship when the building contract was drawn up nothing more could be done about it.

The records of the court of enquiry were kept in great detail and throw considerable light on the methods of ship construction and equipment during the early seventeenth century. Throughout this period Dutch shipbuilding techniques were used extensively in all European countries. No drawings were made; master shipbuilders such as Hybertsson designed directly from the customer's specifications. The king had dictated the measurements and to his plans the ship had been built.

In the years that followed the disaster, the strange story of the sunken flagship of the Swedish fleet became a talking point in the quayside taverns of ports along the sea lanes of the world. Adventurers from many countries came to Stockholm to try their skill at salvaging

the *Vasa* and its contents—treasure that lay a mere hundred feet below the surface of the water and little more than a hundred yards from the shore. Probably the great attraction was the prospect of the wealth which, as flagship of the fleet, she was supposed to have carried. Thus the stage was set, the incentive to courage and ingenuity lay in trying to reach the sunken warship for personal gain. But, unlike the treasure ships that lay scattered about the tropic islands of more southerly latitudes where the water was warm and clear, Stockholm harbour is cold and muddy—two strong deterrents to the enthusiasm of early divers.

Within three days of the catastrophe a Briton applied for permission to raise the ship. His name was Ian Bulmer, and he described himself as "Engineer to His Majesty the King of England". His conditions were stipulated: "no cure, no pay". Bulmer's application was accepted by the Council of Ministers, and barely had the memorial service for the drowned victims come to an end, when the first attempt at salvaging the *Vasa* was started. The top of her one hundred and eighty-foot mainmast still protruded at an angle above the water, and Bulmer's first task was to set her on an even keel. Knowledge of the diving-bell had not reached Sweden at that time: diving suits with breathing apparatus did not exist until the nineteenth century. How Bulmer succeeded in the first part of his task is not known. It may be assumed that strong ropes were attached to the three masts at some short distance below the surface of the water and that teams of many horses supplied the necessary pulling power. Resistance from the mud in those early days would not have been great as *Vasa*

had not had time to bed herself deeply. The horse power available was unlimited, the ship was brought on to an even keel, and that was the sum total of Bulmer's achievement. He continued to work from anchored rafts above the *Vasa* using grappling-irons, which he hoped would engage in the open gun-ports. Whatever process of winching-up was resorted to brought no reward and only served to damage the superstructure of the ship.

After this first attempt had failed, the Swedish Navy took on the task, but little progress was recorded.

So began the long period when one salvage idea after another was tried, and a growing collection of lost grappling-irons accumulated on the deck and round the base of the *Vasa*. With every fresh attempt at salvage the same frustrating failures resulted. Each company that tried served only to wrench off more carvings, which, being waterlogged, sank into the mud. As the years became decades the old ship settled deeper, with her treasures about her, into the clay.

In 1652 a Scotsman, Colonel Alexander Forbes, applied for a permit to work on the *Vasa* project, and for several years continued, with little success. It was during this period that Hans Albrecht von Treileben, a soldier of fortune, returned to Sweden from service with the army in Europe. He was fascinated by the problems of underwater work, and accepted, as his predecessors had done, the challenge of the sunken *Vasa*. He reached Stockholm in 1658, bringing with him a knowledge of the diving-bell. But Alexander Forbes was still in command of salvage operations, so von Treileben set about the work of recovering

cannons from a ship which had settled outside Gothenburg harbour to a similar depth to that of the *Vasa*.

With the success of this venture to his credit, von Treileben returned to Stockholm determined to try out his diving-bell on the *Vasa*. The prospect of raising her valuable bronze cannon after thirty years' submersion was now at last a practical possibility. But Forbes still had the salvage rights and would not relinquish them.

Then a successful German diver, Andreas Peckell, arrived on the scene, and Forbes, whose work had achieved nothing more than contributing fresh damage to the *Vasa's* upperworks, was finally squeezed out by the united efforts of von Treileben and Peckell. On 27th August 1663 the two newcomers were granted the right of salvage.

So, thirty-five years after the disaster, really new salvage techniques were to be used and the diving-bell was brought by road from Gothenburg to Stockholm. The sleeping *Vasa* was to have no peace.

The arrival of von Treileben's bell must have created a special stir among the quayside loafers, for such a thing had never been seen before.

It seems strange that in the seventeenth-century, when so many rich rewards were being won by the use of the diving-bell in salvage works on sunken galleons in other parts of the world, it had not been tried at an earlier date on the *Vasa*. Sweden at that time was a world power, trade with Europe was constant, and knowledge of the diving-bell and its success must have reached the country.

As early as 350 B.C. Aristotle refers to a kind of kettle

by which divers could supply themselves with fresh air under water.

The year 1250 is traditionally believed to be the date when the diving-bell was invented by Roger Bacon.

In 1538 John Tasnier, who travelled to Africa with King Charles V, relates that he saw "at Toledo, in Spain, two Greeks let themselves down under water in a large inverted kettle".

In 1620 Sir Francis Bacon refers to a "machine used to assist persons labouring under water upon wrecks by affording a reservoir of air".

In 1642, in America, Bedall of Boston used submerged weighted tubs in which he descended to the *Marie Rose*. "The lifting arrangements of the ship were completed by means of diving-bells and the loaded vessel was transported to shoal water."

In 1664 cannons were recovered from wrecks of the Spanish Armada by the Laird of Melgin near the Isle of Man.

In 1666 James Maulde worked from a diving-bell on a Spanish galleon of the Armada sunk in Tobermory bay.

In 1687 £300,000 was recovered with the use of a diving-bell at a depth of seven fathoms from a Spanish ship wrecked near the Bermudas.

In 1688 a diving-bell company was formed in England, and successful descents were made to ships sunk off the coast of Hispaniola.

By the autumn of 1663 negotiations for the transfer of Colonel Forbes's *Vasa* salvage contract to von Treileben were complete. Thus at last the stage was set for the first real contact with the *Vasa* since the disastrous evening thirty-five years before.

27

The diving-bell was almost a sphere in shape. It was constructed of lead and inset with circular glass windows. The opening to the water was on the under side. It was taken out to rafts and anchored over the *Vasa*, where it was suspended from a small crane.

When all arrangements were complete, one of the diving team, wearing a watertight leather suit, was assisted onto the heavy standing platform that hung beneath the opening of the bell. It was then hoisted over the water and lowered away. The British diver, James Maulde, who later worked on the Tobermory wreck, made this first descent. As the bell was lowered into the sea the water rose round his legs; he grimaced through the window at the men who worked the crane, and gave them the seventeenth-century equivalent of the thumbs-up sign to lower away. As the minutes dragged by, exceeding the time for which a man could hold his breath, consternation spread among the watchers on the quay, but their concern was tempered by the obvious lack of anxiety shown by von Treileben and his men on the raft, and a strange silence came over the watching scene. The bell continued to descend into the water, and to Maulde the sound of voices on the raft above faded away in the dim silent world of the sea. With every foot of depth the pressure increased on the air trapped in the upper part of the bell in which he breathed, and with inexorable slowness the water rose higher about his body. Gradually his sight became accustomed to the gloom and he was able to distinguish through his circular window the grey-green labyrinth of masts, spars and sagging ropes of the *Vasa* as he sank slowly past them. The tattered remnants of the topsail, which had once

been so proudly set, hung limp and shapeless where it had rotted from the cross-trees, and its ragged bulk lay draped about the lower yard-arm, which was heavily festooned with drooping weed. As the bell continued its descent the water rose as high as Maulde's chest. His ears had been plugged, but the pressure was now great and a high-pitched ringing mingled with the fast throb of his beating heart. Maulde gave a tug at the line which connected with the surface; this was the signal to stop lowering and give him time to acclimatise himself to the rapidly increasing air pressure inside the bell. His breath condensed in a film on the glass window, and he had to wipe it continually to see the fantastic world into which he had entered. On either side, through a labyrinth of sagging tangled shrouds thickened by slime and weed, it was difficult to recognise the once proud cordage of a gallant ship. Shoals of small fish and crustaceans thronged the wreck. As the ringing in his ears and the pounding of his heart eased, Maulde signalled with another tug, and the bell moved into the murk until he could see the deck itself. Everywhere was a grim confusion of broken woodwork and lost grappling tools. The mud and weeds of three and a half decades had settled over everything to disguise the fact that these things were the handwork of man. From the high stern deck the silhouettes of carved gods, kings, knights, reptiles and other shapes looked down at the man who had ventured from above in his tiny leaded cage of air. Most divers of that early superstitious time would have pulled the life-line to signal a quick return to the surface, but James Maulde was an adventurer on the threshold of the scientific age; besides, he was a

treasure seeker and knew that a great reward lay in store for a successful diving team.

The air inside the bell was becoming hot and he knew that soon he would need to signal to be hauled up. Previous experience told him that warning symptoms soon would make him uncomfortable. If he overstayed his time, the first warning would be a tingling sensation on his skin, which would be followed by pains in the joints of arms and legs.

The bell had now settled on the deck and Maulde carefully stepped from his platform and, pressing his hands against the inside of the bell, shuffled across the ship's boards, taking the bell with him, the nearest living counterpart to a hermit crab inside its adopted shell.

The starboard cannons, which had broken loose from their tackles and breechings when the ship heeled over to port, now lay strewn about the larboard side, their wooden carriages in wild confusion. Quickly the diver estimated the chances of their recovery; but even as he looked, the mud which he had disturbed on the deck began to cloud the water about him. The contrast between the warmth of the foul air and the coldness of the water on his leather suit reminded him that time was running out. He stepped back on to the platform inside the bell, gave two sharp pulls on the line, and felt himself rising gently away from the cloud of disturbed mud. He rose steadily past the weed-covered rigging and spars and on and up into the green translucence of the surface water.

When the diving-bell emerged once more into the light of day and was swung onto the raft, von Treileben and Peckell helped Maulde out of his leather suit. The

diver had an acute headache and a choking cough. Warm clothes were put on his shaking body; and when he had recovered sufficiently to make his report, his helpers heard the first account of conditions on the *Vasa's* deck.

In the following spring the real attempt at salvage was started. Relays of divers went down in the leaden bell, and very gradually worthless articles were pushed off the cluttered deck and the first big gun was roped up.

On 1st April 1664 a bronze firing piece was hauled to the surface, and the operation showed every promise of success. By the end of that summer every gun on the *Vasa's* upper deck had been brought up, and von Treileben was planning to get his divers to rip off the boards of the top deck in order to penetrate to the lower gun decks.

By the following year fifty-three of the *Vasa's* full complement of sixty-four cannon had been hauled from the lower decks. How this was achieved from a simple diving bell is beyond the understanding of modern diving experts. It was an underwater epic of courage surpassed only by that of the twentieth-century Swedish diving crew who prepared the way for the old ship's journey to the surface in April 1961.

Since the written account of the export of the fifty-three cannons in the year of their salvage, no further news of the *Vasa* has been found in the archives of the Swedish capital. After the stripping of this valuable armament, interest in her began to wane, and gradually she was forgotten, until all trace of her position was lost and her name, like the dynasty of the Vasa kings, passed into the dust of history.

31

CHAPTER 2

The Great Discovery

THE discovery of the *Vasa* in 1956 was the result of a long dedicated quest by a man whose early dreams of discovering lost galleons persisted from boyhood through to adult life. Most boys dream of finding buried treasure, but few do anything about it; fewer still have the tenacity to continue searching long after youthful enthusiasm has died away.

But to Swedish-born Anders Franzén the dream had become an obsession. Fortunately for him (and for Sweden), his parents owned a summer house on an island in that wonderful archipelago where the waters of Stockholm merge into the Baltic Sea. The family owned a motor launch. These were the circumstances which were to provide the opportunity that led to one of the great marine archaeological discoveries of the twentieth century.

By 1945, when Franzén was in his middle twenties, he was already meticulously searching the Stockholm archipelago for whatever secrets of the period of Sweden's greatness lay buried between the islands along the shallow Baltic seaboard. Throughout the summer Franzén spent long weekends questing from island to island in his launch. He used an assortment of sounding devices and dragnets, and was always talking to fishermen and

A decorative portrait bust, probably of Neptune. One of the finds brought up by the divers, after it has been hosed down on the raft.

The Vasa *sheaf and crown, afterwards found to be part of the Royal Coat of Arms decorating the ship's stern, receiving first-aid treatment. In the background a number of other finds are covered with wet sacking to prevent the timbers from drying out and opening.*

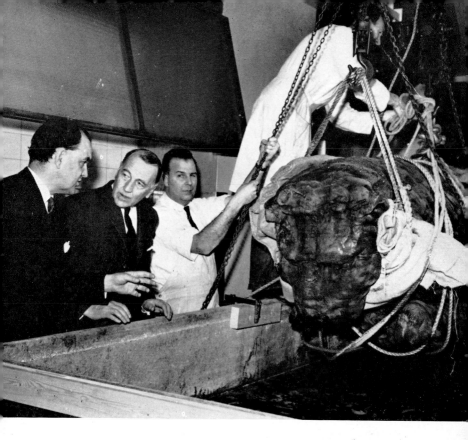

The *two-and-a-half-ton* lion figurehead from the Vasa, *here being lowered steadily, face downwards, into a bath of glycol at the Preservation Centre.*

Dr. Lars Barkman at work in the Preservation Centre, where part of an ancient gun carriage is being lowered into the tank of glycol.

Butter from a seventeenth-century churn, and almost edible. It was claimed that only a slight rancidity had set in to upset the flavour of this 330-year-old keg of butter which had been preserved in the mud.

One of the lion masks that decorated the inside of the gun-port lids. When one of these lids was open the lion mask stared out beside the cannon's mouth and was intended to add to the terror of the enemy. The first one that was brought up was immediately adopted as a mascot by the modern salvors.

An earthenware cooking-pot, glazed on the inside. Cooking arrangements were of the most primitive form; being in a wooden ship, the danger from fire precluded all but the simplest forms of cooking.

A water bottle.

A wooden jug.

The leather boot of a long-dead sailor, who was drowned as the Vasa *sank.*

sailors, gradually building up in his mind a plan for ultimate success.

He found several old wrecks of sunken wooden ships. He formed a theory that *Teredo navalis*, the "death-watch beetle" of the sea which destroys the woodwork of ships submerged in normal sea-water, did not exist in the more brackish water of the Baltic.

Teredo navalis has a slender worm-like body of up to twelve inches in length; the rasping action of its file-like shell valves at the head enables it to bore. No timber is immune from its attack. It bores with extra-ordinary speed, usually along the grain of the wood, and however crowded the tunnels may become they never run into each other. If the wall of a burrow is breached the teredo dies. Research has shown that one hundred million eggs can be shed by a female during a year. At the point where the larvae enter the surface of the wood no more than a pinhole is visible so that timber which may appear in good condition on the outside can be virtually eaten away within. The life of untreated timber may be only one year in some regions.

In the third century B.C. the Greeks used lead sheathing to protect their ships. In the reign of Charles II it was ordered that lead sheath be used on naval vessels. By 1761 wooden ships were sheathed with copper below the waterline. Bridges on untreated timber piers have collapsed, wharves have subsided and ships have been sunk by the action of teredo. The havoc wrought on the woodwork of dykes in eighteenth-century Holland often led to breaching by the sea and extensive damage from flooding over the low countries.

Franzén's theory was correct. The teredo was not present in those waters. So he continued his search, with the growing conviction that he would some day find a famous ship of the line in good condition and in a convenient place for lifting and preservation—perhaps even the fabled *Vasa* of which his father had often told him.

One by one Franzén located the positions of the *Grone Jagaren* (The Green Huntsman), the *Riksapplet* (The Orb of the Realm), the *Riksvasa* (The Vasa Realm), and the *Riksnyckeln* (The Key of the Realm). The timbers of these seventeenth-century ships, although damaged by current and tide, were all untouched by the teredo, and Franzén became even more certain that the *Vasa*, which had sunk in calm fresh water where the great lake of Malaren passes through Stockholm harbour, must also be in good condition.

Gradually he spent more time on searching the harbour water in the hope of striking the oak of the *Vasa*.

As the years went by, young Anders ignored the call of material advancement in the Swedish oil company for which he worked. His widowed mother, with whom he lived, often chided him for his lack of ambition as she saw his colleagues climbing the ladder ahead of him. Sometimes his work took him overseas—he came to Britain: Swansea, Cardiff, Portsmouth and London— but on returning home the quest for his country's long-lost galleons was always taken up with fresh enthusiasm.

Throughout the winter nights he worked at the city archives reading through ancient manuscripts of the period after the *Vasa's* sinking in the hope of finding a

clue that would help him to locate her resting-place. He studied and mastered the old Swedish language of the period in order to read the hand-written records of some four hundred years before.

Years passed, and Anders Franzén kept to his self-imposed task with a dedication that was bound to lead to success. The old saying that "nothing is denied to well-directed labour" has never been more clearly exemplified than in the grim determination of this amateur archæologist. Throughout the summer months his spare time was taken up by his growing obsession to find the *Vasa*. As the evenings shortened at the approach of the Scandinavian winter he transferred his attention once again to puzzling through the records of ancient Stockholm. On one occasion in 1954 he came upon a reference to the *Vasa*, and with the help of his magnifying glass he slowly deciphered the old script. The place of her sinking was vaguely described as "behind Lustholmen, this side of Blockhusudden, by Danviken". It was not very helpful, but sufficient to inspire him with renewed determination. When the lighter evenings returned he continued searching from his motorboat *Dolaro*, taking soundings with his heavy-core sampler, but the wooden walls of the ancient man-o'-war still eluded him.

During the next winter he found an eighteenth-century map of the harbour, which had been used by a previous wreck hunter who had also tried to find the *Vasa*. The map was marked with a cross by a place called Stadsgardskajen; it suggested that this was the spot where the *Vasa* had sunk.

During the summer of 1955 Franzén confined his

search to this area, taking thousands of soundings, but he found nothing. Friends began to question his sanity in keeping on with it; others thought that during his search of the archives he had discovered records of some great treasure which the ship had carried, and that his relentless quest was inspired by the hope of "easy money". Franzén had found no clues to great treasure. The genuine love of marine archaeology, which he practised with the enthusiasm of the devoted amateur for a favourite hobby, was the driving force. Professional archaeologists regarded him with suspicion and disfavour, but he was unworried by what others thought or said about him.

Then in the winter of 1956 he uncovered the clue he had sought so long. It was the original letter the Council of the Realm had sent to King Gustavus Adolphus two days after the disaster. The letter contained details of the sinking of the *Vasa* and the exact place where she had foundered. ". . . and this past Sunday, as stated, shortly after evensong . . . the wind south-west and the weather calm . . . and when she came out into the bay by Tegelviken there came more wind into her sails . . . came to Beckholmsudden, where she entirely fell on her side. . . ."

Beckholm, the little island which Franzén knew so well! In that one place-name he knew that his long search was nearly over.

One can have little conception of the significance of that discovery to this man who had quested blindly for so long into the muddy depths of the complicated harbour of Stockholm. The excitement of that one discovery was as great as the wonders yet to come.

Franzén began sounding the harbour floor off Beckholm island with his core sampler. This was a weighty metal instrument which plummeted down into the water at the end of a line. Three tail vanes ensured its vertical descent. The forward end consisted of a sharp-edged hollow tube. On striking wood it would pierce the surface and core out a sample for inspection after being returned to the boat. During August 1956 Franzén felt the instrument bore into a hard surface and quickly hauled it up. A piece of ancient black oak was visible in the ferrule of his instrument. He tried again and again, and each time he drew up a piece of dark oak from the water. He was barely a hundred yards off the entrance to a small dry dock on the island of Beckholm, and he felt certain that he was at last directly over the ancient wreck of the *Vasa*. After noting its position, he took his boat ashore and hurried off to the Commanding Officer of the Naval Diving School. His excitement was infectious, and together they decided to hold the School's routine tests for trainee divers at the place where he had struck the ancient oaken ship.

The diving launch was taken to the spot, and Anders Franzén watched as the powerfully built chief diver, Per Edvin Falting, was prepared by his assistants for the first descent to the wooden hulk below. When the watertight diving dress was fitted, together with the weighted boots and belt weights, the helmet was lifted, put over his head and screwed down on the corslet. Then Falting stepped heavily through the special opening in the stern of the launch and, like his predecessors of three centuries earlier, prepared for his descent to the wreck below. This time the diver was

helped by the cumulative knowledge of scientific progress after more than four hundred years. He breathed
fresh air brought by pipeline from the compressor. He
had a life-line, telephone, and submarine electric lamp.

His disappearance beneath the murky water caused
no concern to the salvage crew, only a tinge of jealousy
that the chief should have the privilege of making the
first dive. The main concern felt by everyone, and
most particularly by Anders Franzén, was the prob-
ability of what the dive would reveal—if anything!
There was no guarantee that they were on to the *Vasa*;
the oak found in the core sampler could have been
from a sunken ketch of no interest to anyone.

What could have been Franzén's feelings as he
watched the bubbles bursting near the stern of the
launch? He stared into the muddy blackness of the
water. Some minutes elapsed, then—almost unex-
pectedly—the diver's voice came over the loud-speaker:
"I'm now lowering myself down beside a wreck. It's
very dark, but I can feel a square opening in the hull.
Here's another one, and another . . ."

To Franzén this was the realisation of his dream. At
that moment something told him he had found the
Vasa. The square openings could only be the gun-
ports of an ancient man-o'-war. It *must* be the *Vasa*,
the long-lost flagship of the great imperial fleet.

As Falting continued to explore the ship with the
aid of his lamp, he gave a running commentary for the
benefit of the listeners on the launch above. As the
powerful beam cut into the darkness he could see the
remnants of the fantastic sterncastle rising out of the
mud, badly damaged by the groping and dragging of

the early salvage teams but still recognisable. A labyrinth of lost anchors and grapples complicated things for Falting, and, encumbered by his heavy diving outfit, he moved only with great difficulty. Besides the damage inflicted by the early salvagers, ships had anchored in the wreck's vicinity; their anchors had caught in the *Vasa's* woodwork and had torn it loose. Three centuries of such treatment had wrought havoc on the superstructure, and gradually her ornate finery had been stripped away, to settle in the mud and be covered by the silt of centuries. Falting continued his inspection, climbing over spars, girders, anchors, statues and carvings; all the while his beam revealed fresh wonders in that silent grave world of the sleeping ship. The towering wooden walls rose up beside him, and from some of the gun-ports on the lower deck the muzzles of ancient cannons peeped. The ship was the *Vasa*. But the *Vasa* was dead; this was the blackened, broken corpse of the fluttering argosy which had proudly set her sails on a voyage of conquest.

Then the listeners above heard the diver formally take possession of the ship on behalf of the crown.

In 1961 I visited Stockholm and spoke to Edvin Falting. I asked him what his feelings were when he first stood on the *Vasa's* deck. His reply was characteristic. His feelings, he said, were of unlimited admiration and amazement at the courage of von Treileben's men in being able to dislodge and raise fifty-three two-ton cannons from the lower decks while standing inside a primitive diving-bell. He said that he felt privileged to be the first man to stand where they had stood.

After Falting's first commentary from the bed of the

harbour, news of the discovery quickly reached the city. Anders Franzén received the congratulations of the crew, and subsequently of the press, television and the Swedish public. The king, himself an enthusiastic archaeologist, gave Franzén a royal congratulation. Franzén was alone no longer, he was the toast of his country's capital, and the story of his discovery was given world-wide publicity. Far-sighted people started planning for the future. The find was treated as one of major significance, for Swedish archaeologists realised that here lay an early seventeenth-century ship in a good state of preservation and still containing many of the objects with which she had been provided for her maiden voyage. She was regarded as a complete inventory of the life of her day, and of inestimable value to the city and the nation.

The real significance of the *Vasa* discovery lay in the fact that no records of naval ship architecture exist from the first half of the seventeenth century. Little was known about ship design until the 1670s, as no drawings were committed to paper, or at least no such records existed, and no models exist in maritime museums. The earliest record is Edward Battine's notebook of calculations, which was made in 1684 and can be seen in the British Maritime Museum at Greenwich. Battine classified all ships as being from the first to the sixth rate; corresponding measurements are laid down for each of the six rates. So the finding of the *Vasa* is of great importance to students of early shipbuilding. The *Vasa* is acknowledged to be the oldest fully identified ship in the world, and, in addition, she is a treasure-house of antiquities from a period of which

little existed in the museums of Sweden. The significance of the words of Philippe Diolé must have been fully appreciated; he said: "An ancient shipwreck is a complete inventory and the most crystal-clear and concentrated report concerning the culture at the time of the disaster. It is only on board a ship, where so many testifying things are gathered together in a small space, that an entire cross-section of life can suddenly be arrested and preserved by the sea."

The oldest fully identified ship hitherto had been Admiral Nelson's flagship, the *Victory*, now preserved in Portsmouth harbour. This ship gives a clear picture of design and fittings from the date of 1805. The *Vasa* antedates Trafalgar by nearly two centuries. Egyptian burial ships have been unearthed, and Roman ceremonial galleys of Lake Nemi have been found; these are very much older, of course, than *Vasa*, but, like the Norwegian Oseberg and Gokstad Viking galleys preserved at Bygdoy in Oslo, they are ceremonial vessels which are not fully identified and play little part in filling the gap in our knowledge of the evolution of ship construction.

From the diver's reports it was obvious that the woodwork was in a good state of preservation, but because of the immense weight of mud which had settled on the decks and in the hold there was no means of knowing whether she would stand the strain of being lifted. She was upright, but buried to her original water-line in mud and clay. She had suffered no ill effects from fire, explosion, enemy gun-fire, rough seas, tide action or marine parasitic life, as in the case of other sunken galleons. Her resting-place in the tranquil

41

harbour water, so close to the naval dockyard, could hardly have been more convenient for salvage. But even with so many favourable aspects to the problem of raising the *Vasa*, it was only the salvage experts who realised the enormity of the task that lay ahead. They knew that if the ship was to be brought to the surface in one piece it would take considerable time and much expense. The news of the discovery was too sudden and too big for any immediate decisions to be taken, and it was wisely decided not to rush the excavation.

In the following year the Vasa Committee was formed, with Commodore Edward Clason as chairman. The committee was instructed to investigate every aspect involved with the salvage of the ship. After prolonged deliberations the committee issued a directive worthy of the great "Northern Hurricane" himself: "Raise the *Vasa*."

CHAPTER 3

"Raise the Vasa"

C HIEF diver Edvin Falting first boarded the ship
under water in September 1956, but with the onset
of autumn events moved slowly. It was found that the
sixty-foot foremast was still in position; it hampered the
early work of the divers, so it was detached, removed by
crane, and deposited on the island of Beckholm.

Then in January the Vasa Committee was formed and
made the final decision to go ahead. It was obvious
that if it had been possible to lift her immediately, her
timbers would quickly crack and warp because of rapid
drying in the atmosphere after her long submersion. It
was therefore decided to keep her under water until a
suitable house could be built to receive her; this would
have to be a building in which the humidity could be
controlled and a gradual drying-out process maintained
over a period of several years.

But to lift her immediately was of course an impossi-
bility, and the administrators of the project planned for
a salvage job that would take several years, by which
time, it was hoped, a special Vasa Museum would be
ready to receive and protect her from the air.

The problem involved in overcoming the suction of
the deep bed of clay in which she had settled was one of
the first considerations. Many salvage experts were

consulted, and many bold and highly imaginative suggestions were submitted to the committee for her recovery. One idea was that she should be crammed with millions of table-tennis balls which would eventually bring her to the surface. Another, perhaps more serious proposition was that of freezing the water inside her until she became a solid block of ice, when she would float to the surface like an iceberg. But the committee finally decided to accept the suggestion that the normal conventional practice of wreck lifting by using two large pontoons should be tried. The lowering and raising of the pontoons should gradually bring the *Vasa* to the surface.

It was fortunate that the Neptun Salvage Company had two enormous pontoons, the *Oden* and *Frigg*, which had been built in 1898 to raise a Russian battleship sunk in the Baltic. The use of these was offered to the committee.

The plan was to pass strong steel cables under the *Vasa* which would then be suspended from the two pontoons. By lowering and raising the pontoons, the *Vasa*, cradled below, would gradually be brought to the surface. But before the cables could be passed under the ship six tunnels would need to be dug beneath her keel.

This tunnelling would be a hazardous job. The work was taken up by Edvin Falting and four petty officers of the Royal Swedish Navy. To Lennart Carlbom, Ragnar Jansson, Sven-Olof Nyberg, and Stig Friberg, together with their chief, must go the honour of accomplishing this feat demanding cold-blooded courage.

New diving operations started in the spring of 1957, and from the gloomy depths one fascinating object after

another was hauled to the surface. Commodore Edward Clason, the committee chairman, was also personally in charge of the diving operations, and his was the task of numbering and cataloguing the finds as they were brought up. There was special excitement when the beautifully carved port-side headrail was hauled on to the diving raft. It represented a superb example of the preservative qualities of the mud, and was an indication of the wealth of ornamental splendour that was to follow. In the mud round the bow and stern the relics of the old ship's superstructure, together with dozens of anchors and grapples of varying ages, lay together as in some forgotten junk yard of history.

Before tunnelling could be started each loose object was sent to the surface, numbered, catalogued, washed and submerged in tanks of water on the island to be kept wet. The number of tanks steadily increased, and when the supply of tanks ran out huge wooden boxes were made and disused house baths were used. Every piece of broken timber was treated with as much care as if it were a beautiful carving.

As the summer of 1957 advanced, all relics were cleared from the mud on either side of the bow, and preparations were made for starting the first tunnel.

The ship had settled into the clay bed of the harbour to a depth of eight feet; above this lay a deposit of semi-organic black mud for another eight feet up to the region of the *Vasa's* original water-line.

The tool used for excavating the tunnels was the Zetterstrom-jet, an invention of Arne Zetterstrom (who broke the world's deep-diving record with his descent to five hundred and twenty-eight feet in 1945). His

method involves the use of a powerful jet of water which cuts into the clay; the recoil action of the forward jet is counteracted by a series of smaller jets which are directed backwards from behind the nozzle. The excavated mud and clay is drawn off along a six-inch hosepipe by an air-lift mud-suction device. Compressed air is blown into the lower end, and the resulting mixture of air, water and mud is drawn away upwards and ejected.

No one knew whether it would succeed in this instance; few people understood the difficulties of the project, and only the divers themselves realised fully the dangers involved. Clad in their cumbersome diving outfits, they would be suspended upside-down in complete blackness burrowing almost vertically downwards through mud for sixteen feet until the keel was reached.

By 9th September everything was ready for the start of the excavation. The mud-suction air-lift pipe was in position, the compressor was started, and the soft detritious mud of the surface began to be drawn away.

At this stage an exciting new find was made: the magnificently carved mask of a lion's head which had decorated one of the gun-port lids was recovered from the mud. After washing, traces of the original gold leaf still adhered to it in places. The new find was considered as a good omen for the success of the project.

When the hollow formed by the air-lift pipe was big enough, the first diver lowered himself down through the water and into the hole, taking the Zetterstrom-jet with him. In spite of the brilliant light from his lamp, he could see little beyond the glass window in his helmet. Because of the difficult and restricted field of operations

46

each diver had to return to the surface after only fifteen minutes. Then the next man would descend into the mud hole to re-apply the jet and loosen more mud, which was automatically blown backwards. One diver after another lowered himself down through the hundred feet of water to the old ship's side; then, feeling his way head downwards along the suction pipes into the soft mud hole until he came to the Zetterstrom-jet head, he would switch on the power and cutting could be resumed for another fifteen minutes. No diver knew whether tons of mud might give way and avalanche in upon him and seal him up in a muddy tomb. The chance of being able to dig himself out even with the help of the jet was very remote. It was a case of blinding on and on in the darkness until the extreme discomfort made the diver switch off and wriggle out of the hole, to return to the surface and wait until each one of the other members of the crew had done his stint.

As the tunnel went deeper the clay hardened and progress slowed down. Autumn turned to winter, and by 10th December it was decided to cease further activities until the following spring.

In April 1958 diving was resumed, fresh deposits of mud were blown out by the jet and one at a time the tunnel gang bored down until at last the great keel of the *Vasa* was reached. Then they started from the other side of the ship at a point exactly opposite the first tunnel. The process was repeated until at last the keel was again reached and the first tunnel under the *Vasa* was complete. The date was 6th August 1958, eleven months from the day on which the tunnel had been started.

Then on 5th September the first bronze cannon was

removed from its gun-port and hauled to the surface by a pontoon crane from the naval dockyard. It weighed two thousand five hundred pounds, and had been badly scratched by cables and anchor chains. But the letters G.A.R.S.—Gustavus Adolphus Rex Sueciae—were discernible. Here was the last and final proof that the ship was without any doubt the *Vasa*.

The previous cannon had been brought up in 1683, but how this was achieved from a diving-bell with the primitive tackle of the period remains a mystery. The weight of cannon removed in 1683 totalled seventy tons, and it is thought that this lightening of the ship at that time probably saved it from disintegration and collapse.

Work on the second tunnel proceeded with feverish haste; more powerful compressed air equipment was used, and work was completed by the end of the month. But by December all further diving had to cease once again.

Early in 1959, the year in which the *Vasa* was to leave her three-hundred-and-thirty-year-old grave, two donations were received: one of £6,500 from the Wallenberg Foundation, and another of £2,500 from the Royal Foundation. At a later date £6,500 was donated by Director A. E. Carell. This year, which marked the turning point in the recovery of the old ship, opened with renewed hope and activity for the men who were working on the project.

By the end of May the third tunnel was completed.

With these excavations into the mud at the start of each tunnelling operation interesting finds were continually being made. On 15th May the lower part of the great mainmast (its original height was between 180

48

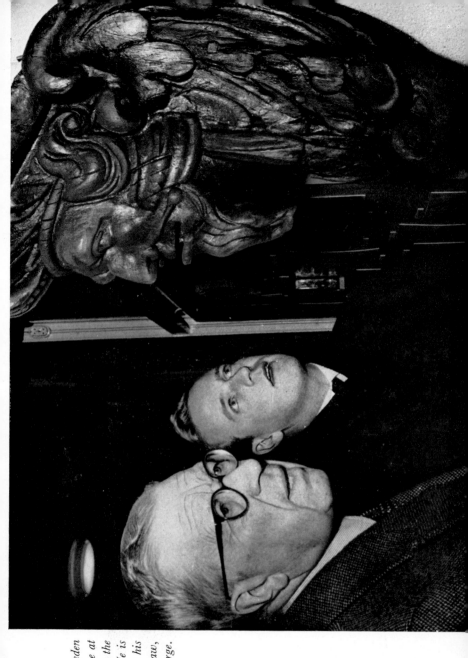

The King of Sweden inspecting a sculpture at the exhibition hall in the Vasa museum. He is accompanied by his son-in-law, Prince Johan George.

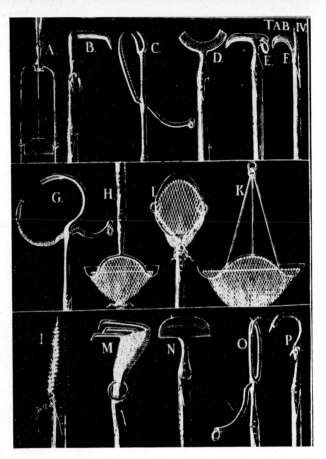

Von Treileben's underwater tools used by his divers to rip off deck planking to reach the cannon for roping up.

Lieut. Commander Bo Cassel being lowered in a modern diving bell to the scene of the Vasa disaster, to demonstrate the seventeenth-century method of cannon fishing, before an audience of 3,000 delegates when the International Historical Congress met at Stockholm in 1960.

The two pontoons being filled with water preparatory to beginning the first lift. The six-inch hawsers have been drawn tight and clamped, after which the pontoons will be pumped empty and, on rising higher out of the water, will draw the Vasa from the harbour bed.

The Neptun salvage fleet with the two pontoons on which the big hydraulic jacks have been mounted preparatory to the last stage in the raising operation, on the day before the lift took place.

On board at last: the supreme moment in the lives of the two men most concerned with the venture. Anders Franzén, the discoverer, and Per Edvin Falting, the chief diver, step on board one of the deck beams as the ship breaks surface. They were treated to a great ovation from the vast crowd assembled to watch this historic event, and are seen here acknowledging the cheers.

The big hydraulic jacks continue to lift the Vasa and the great submersible pumps begin to discharge the water from the leaking hull.

One of the submersible pumps working at maximum power to overcome the leakages as the Vasa is drawn slowly into port.

The seventeenth-century galleon afloat on her own keel in the port of Stockholm. The pontoons have brought her to the entrance to the dry dock, from which she must make the journey in on her own. Bow and stern have been boxed in by the divers; she still leaks badly but the submersible pumps work furiously to keep her afloat. ▶

The Vasa *in dry dock.*

and 190 feet) was recovered. New finds continued to break surface as wooden pulley blocks, deadeyes, anchors, capstans, the tail of the figurehead lion, the headrail with a figure of Triton the wind god, a splendid carving of Hercules symbol of strength, with Cerberus the hell dog, the enormous oak bracket which supported the bowsprit, and numerous knights and figurines, followed each other in quick succession. A coat of arms with the Vasa sheaf supported by cherubs appeared, with red paint and gold leaf still visible on the carved woodwork. More lion-head masks from the gun-port lids, mermaids, animals, and carved heads, with a wealth of ornament, were recovered.

One of the most amusing finds was a keg of butter, which, although three hundred and thirty years old, was only slightly rancid. The beer barrels contained a liquid from which all trace of the smell of their former contents had long since departed. The beer had been brewed while Shakespeare was writing, and its lack of flavour was not surprising. But the brandy, so I was informed, was still palatable.

In spite of the fact that tunnelling was frequently held up by these continual finds, the divers continued their work with mounting confidence and efficiency. The fourth tunnel was completed by 5th June, 1959, and the fifth tunnel by 8th July, and by the end of that month the sixth and last tunnel was finished. Then the last of the guide wires was passed from the diving rafts under the keel of the *Vasa* and she was secured.

This remarkable salvage operation is regarded as an underwater achievement unparalleled in the history of diving. During the whole project one thousand five

hundred hours had been spent under water by the divers in conditions of bitter cold and absolute blackness: in positions of extreme discomfort, and in constant danger of mud displacement and death. Now the most dangerous part of the job was over, the ship was a cradled captive awaiting the arrival of the salvage fleet and its two great pontoons.

Then on 5th August, as though to set the seal on this superb achievement, the ship's giant figurehead, the Vasa lion, was brought up. Crowds of people gathered round the harbour to see it break surface.

It had been built in sections of linden wood, and as the mud was hosed away, the gold leaf on the deeply carved mane brought gasps of admiration from the watchers. As these traces of the splendour of this ancient battle galleon of the days of sail were revealed, the watchers must have felt something of the words inscribed on the dry-dock wall of the *Cutty Sark* at Greenwich:

"They mark our passage as a race of men,
　　Earth shall not see such ships as these again."

On 12th August, six days after the completion of the last tunnel, the salvage vessels arrived beside the diving rafts on which so many early seventeenth-century relics had been first revealed. The lifting pontoons were anchored on either side of the line of rafts, and auxiliary salvage vessels took up positions outside the pontoons. Pumping was started almost immediately, and the pontoons were filled with water until their upper decks were nearly awash. Then the temporary cables which had been taken through the tunnels under the *Vasa*

50

were substituted by heavy six-inch steel hawsers which would have to take the immense strain of the first lift. Four thousand five hundred feet of hawser was used.

When these were in position under the hull, and the ends were locked together on the pontoon decks by heavy giant clips, the big lift was ready to begin.

By 20th August they started pumping the water out of the pontoons. Gradually they rose higher out of the water, the locked hawsers took the strain, and the harbour mud began to release the great wooden hull which it had held for nearly three and a half centuries.

Diver Sven-Olof Nyberg put on his under-water suit and descended to the *Vasa's* stern. He reported that she had left her bed and risen two feet. There was great jubilation on the pontoons' decks as the news was broadcast over the loud-speaker. Pumping continued, the pontoons rose higher and the calculated seven hundred tons weight of the submerged galleon was lifted clear of her ancient grave. So confident were the salvage experts at this early stage in the operation that the two pontoons were turned round, swinging the suspended *Vasa* with them, until her bow was pointing towards the sheltered waters of Castle Island. Then very slowly the whole flotilla began moving in the direction of the island, the ground sloped gently upwards, and after about a hundred yards the *Vasa* was carefully grounded.

Between 20th August and 16th September eighteen lifts were made and the old ship was moved about a quarter of a mile to comparatively shallow water to await the further development of plans for her future.

Thus ended the first part of the *Vasa* story, with the old ship at this stage resting in nine fathoms of water

in a protected inlet of Kastellholmen. From the office of the Governor of Stockholm came an order prohibiting any unauthorised persons from approaching the site where the *Vasa* lay. It was quite obvious to every one of the vast crowd that thronged the slopes of Kastellholmen that she could have been brought to the surface in that September 1959, and many must have wondered why most of the work was suspended. But to the men who had given so much time and thought to the raising and preservation of the ship time did not matter. They knew that it would be disastrous to bring her out of the water and expose her sodden timbers to the quick-drying action of the air.

Before she would be allowed to break surface many difficulties had still to be overcome, greater difficulties even than the task of bringing her up. It was now an established certainty that the galleon could be raised in one piece and eventually become a world showpiece. This induced the Swedish Government to form a board whose mission was to preserve the ship for posterity. The members are: Chairman, His Royal Highness Prince Bertil; Vice-Chairman, Carl Albert Anderson, Chairman of Stockholm City Council; Gosta Selling, Director-General of the Central Office of National Antiquities; Gunnar Jedeur-Palmgren, Director of the Royal Swedish Naval Administration; Hans Hansson, Curator of the National Maritime Museum; Bengt Petri, Chancellor of the Swedish Universities; Anders Franzén, Royal Swedish Naval Administration; Sven Backlund, Head of the Information Division of the Ministry of Foreign Affairs. Directly responsible to the board is its managing director, Fred Arnell.

In February 1959 a special exhibition of all the *Vasa* treasures was arranged in the National Maritime Museum. It was opened by Their Majesties King Gustav VI Adolf and Queen Louise. The exhibition consisted of four thousand objects, making the most remarkable exhibition ever held in Sweden.

In the following year the Government contributed a substantial grant towards the resumption of work and diving was continued. It was now decided to start repairing her under water so that on surfacing she could be floated and enter the dock on her own keel. This entailed making her watertight by sealing up all gun ports, the damaged stern had to be repaired, and all the holes where the iron nails had rusted away were to be plugged.

Thus the summer of 1960 was spent in the monotonous under-water job of corking up, shoring with planks, nailing, bolting and plugging up the ravages of time.

For his outstanding part in the operation Edvin Falting was decorated by the king with the award of the Vasa Medal. The Royal Order of the Vasa was instituted in 1772 by King Gustav III. On one side it has the three crowns, and on the other the ancient Vasa sheaf. The other members of the tunnel team were also decorated for their outstanding contribution towards the restoration of the ship.

CHAPTER 4

Two Thousand Historians Watch Cannon Fishing, Seventeenth-century Style

IT was a fortuitous piece of luck that a Stockholm journalist Lars Widding, of the newspaper *Expressen* while researching in the Royal Library for his book on the *Vasa*, came upon a fascinating record of early diving. He discovered a seventeenth-century book written by an Italian priest, Francesco Negri, as a result of his travels in Scandinavia. One part of the book describes his visit to the scene of von Treileben's diving operations on the *Vasa*. From Lars Widding's twentieth-century discovery in the library comes Francesco Negri's uninhibited picture of the event. The worthy priest's writing is unhampered by any knowledge of such minor details as oxygen, the variations of pressure, and decompression sickness, for such things were unrecognised in 1663.

"Stockholm (October 1663). Having learned that someone had discovered how to descend comfortably and without risk into the depths of the ocean, I made for the place where this invention was to be found in order to study it—and I can report with satisfaction the following:

One day my patron, the Resident, and I—in company with some of the Resident's friends here in Stockholm—boarded a small boat which had been put at our disposal, and sailed thereupon about one Italian mile out into the gulf, or skerries, to a place where many years ago a ship had capsized and gone to the bottom with men and all. Here we passed over to a large boat where, on the orders of the Resident, the diving work was being carried out in the following manner.

The man who was to be sunk to the bed of the ocean sat down, whereupon a ring or band some two fingers in width was passed over one of his feet and fastened just above the knee. The man now drew on a top boot which, on account of its length, came up over the ring. Two men fastened the top boot by tying a rope several times round it.

A similar procedure was carried out on the other leg, after which a third ring—larger than the two previous ones—was passed over the man's head and shoulders and down on to his waist.

Over all this he donned a pair of coarse leather stockings and a jerkin of similar material. Weights were fastened to the waist and leg rings.

Finally his head was protected by a hood of ordinary cloth, which the man refrained from pulling down to the shoulders so that it remained like a hat.

Ready to begin work, the diver now arose and went with clumsy steps down on to the raft which was made of logs and reminded me of those that we use on our rivers. On the raft there was a five palmi [approx. four feet] high lead bell, to the top part of which was

55

fastened a rope. With the assistance of a block and tackle which was supported by two pieces of timber the bell could be lifted up by a couple of men. When it had been lifted somewhat more than the height of a man the fully-equipped diver stepped up on to the lead platform. This platform was fastened to the bell like a clapper—or else it had been fixed by making four holes in the lower rim of the bell, through which rope was passed and attached firmly to the four corners of the lead platform.

In this way the platform hung down two palmi [one and a half feet] under the bell. The man was then handed a wooden stave, somewhat thinner than a pikestaff and two or three braccia in length [i.e. between four and six feet]. An iron hook was fixed to one end of the stave and with this the man was able to catch at objects which he discovered.

Now the bell with the man inside was swung out over the water and lowered all the way down to the ocean bed. The depth here is that of sixteen men, which fact I ascertained by letting down a line.

When I had observed all this and worked out for myself how the man was able to stay under the water for as much as half an hour I requested—when the bell was returned to the surface—that I might myself be permitted to make a descent in the bell in the same manner.

The unhappy Resident advised me against this and pointed out that while this man succeeded on account of his experience, I should not be able to manage it since it was not my profession.

I explained to him why the man was able to stay under water for such a long time and pointed out that this had nothing whatsoever to do with skill. The explanation is thus:

When the bell first touches the water a certain amount runs in, partly because the bell is bound to touch the surface at a slight angle and partly because of the movement of the waves. A further reason is that the air which is trapped in the bell is cooled by the water and compressed, so that it takes up less room than previously.

According to the teachings of the philosophers concerning the impenetrability of a body, however, the water cannot entirely fill the bell, which fact is simply demonstrated if one immerses a glass mouth downwards in a fluid.

The diver comes right down to the bottom because the other men know how far down they have to lower him. But the first time, before they knew the depth, the diver had to give a sign by pulling on a thin rope with one hand, which went out under the rim of the bell up to the raft.

The diver has no difficulty in seeing down there in the depths, since the sun's rays are sufficient to shine down through the water.

After having been under water for a good fifteen minutes the man gave the sign to be hoisted up again. With the help of his hooked stave he had gripped on to a thick oak plank to which were fastened large, heavy pieces of iron. Through an interpreter I asked the diver if he could have stayed down longer than fifteen minutes.

A half an hour at the most, no longer, was the reply. The reason for this, I believe (I forgot to ask him), is that, through breathing, the air in the bell becomes far too warm, while the cold becomes increasingly trying to the legs and thighs, which are immersed in the cold water.

The man was shaking as if he were suffering from the ague when he came up, despite the fact that he was born in this country and was strong and accustomed to physical hardships. The reason that I, despite my curiosity, did not allow myself to be submerged to the ocean bed in the bell—which I had resolved to do—was that we were now at the end of October (1663) and I was worried lest I contract some illness, which could scarcely have occurred during the summer."

Had the learned gentleman been permitted to make the descent at that time of the year in those northern waters, it is questionable whether he would have described it with such complacency as "descending comfortably". One rather regrets that he was not permitted to try.

Accompanying Francesco Negri's account was a drawing of the diving-bell used by von Treileben's men, together with diagrams of the tools which the divers used to remove the *Vasa's* deck planking to reach the lower decks and cannons. This gave Lars Widding an idea; he and Anders Franzén designed a diving-bell which was made by Carlstroms Engineering Works, and financed by the *Expressen* newspaper. This took place in great secrecy early in the summer of 1960, and

tests were made in a secluded part of the harbour in order to determine the bell's efficiency. Lt.-Commander Bo Cassel, one of Sweden's most experienced divers and wreckage explorers, was the first to descend. Dressed as a frogman and carrying a breathing mask in case of emergency, he stepped aboard the heavy platform and was lowered away, but in spite of the thick steel sheet of which the bell was made, it refused to sink because of the volume of air trapped inside. Extra weights were added to the standing platform, Cassel stepped aboard and this time the bell sank away out of sight with its human passenger.

Very slowly he was lowered to the bed of the harbour, taking ten minutes over the descent in order to give time to acclimatise himself to the increased pressure. The water level was marked with lipstick on the inside of the bell at various points during the journey.

Throughout the periods of Cassel's submersion the watchers above felt much as Francesco Negri must have felt in 1663.

On returning to the surface, Cassel was examined by a naval doctor and declared perfectly sound, but he was warned to expect the onset of a headache due to breathing too much carbon dioxide. Cassel reported that the water only reached up to his waist instead of to the neck as described by the diver in Francesco Negri's account. He also claimed that he realised more fully what extreme hardships the early divers must have experienced. It is believed in Sweden that they took a gulp of air, swam away from the bell to tether the cannons to suspended ropes, and then returned to the

bell for air. It is questionable whether the pressure at 100 feet depth would make this possible.

Further experiments were conducted by Cassel and the diving-bell crew in absolute secrecy, until the occasion arrived for which this exploit was being prepared.

In August 1960 the International Historical Congress was being held in Stockholm, and two thousand delegates from all parts of the world who attended the congress were treated to an exhibition so fantastic that it is doubtful whether any gathering of historians will ever witness its equal again. For two days they were to be given a ringside seat at a cannon fishing expedition, in the seventeenth-century style.

In order to accommodate such a vast gathering at a convenient point above the discoveries, a beflagged destroyer of the Swedish Navy was brought alongside to act as a grandstand. Every vantage point along the starboard side was occupied and crammed with three thousand spectators as Lt.-Commander Cassel, in frogman's outfit, stepped on to the heavy base of the bell and was swung out over the *Vasa*. When everything was ready, he was lowered gently away and disappeared beneath the surface of the water. Throughout the early part of his submersion he gave a running commentary over the loud-speaker. Then the crowd was thrilled to hear the voice of Cassel speaking from under the water, as this tough and brilliant Swedish sailor gave a vivid account of his experience in fluent Swedish, English, French and German. His words were relayed by Swedish radio direct over the Eurovision network. Drama was added to Cassel's final speech, when it became painfully obvious that his air was running low.

Frogmen were ready on the raft in case of an emergency, but everything went according to plan. When the bell returned to the light of day, and as its lower edges broke the surface of the water, a cloud of steam and carbon dioxide burst from it.

Then the historians saw the raising of a seventeenth-century cannon as it was lifted clear of the water and swung on to one of the rafts for cleaning and inspection. Then an enormous anchor appeared, for other divers were hard at work down below, roping up the discoveries. Next followed a heavy gun carriage, which was carefully landed on the raft and immediately trundled away on its cumbersome wheels by a group of modern Swedish sailors in the manner of their earlier compatriots. History was being remade before the astonished gaze of the historians.

Speeches were made from a lecture rostrum, the front of which was decorated with a carved gun-port lion mask. Anders Franzén's description of his method of discovery received a great ovation from the crowded deck of the destroyer. Amateur archaeologist though he was, on that great day he was the talk of the world's leading archaeologists. It was no more than a rightful reward for his unflagging enthusiasm and dedication.

CHAPTER 5

The Ship Breaks Surface

THROUGHOUT 1960 the routine work of making
the *Vasa* hull comparatively watertight was carried
out under water by the divers in the sheltered cove of
Castle Island. Thousands of oak pegs were driven into
holes where the iron nails had rusted away. Each gun-
port was sealed up by wooden covers which were clamped
to the ship's side by hook bolts; a padding between the
modern gun-port lids and the black hull helped to reduce
leaks.

The high stern had been badly damaged by ships
dragging their anchors, and this presented a more
difficult problem to the diving team working fifty feet
below the surface. A substantial wall of planks had to be
nailed onto the stern, and another similar wall round
the upper part of the bow where the bowsprit, lion
figurehead, bracket and headrails had been torn off.
There was no hurry at this stage, and the naval divers,
now assisted by frogmen, made a thorough job of sealing
the main leaks.

Meanwhile much thought was given to the best
method of displaying the *Vasa* for the benefit of posterity.

It was by a unique stroke of coincidence that this
culturally important wreck should have been discovered

barely a quarter of a mile from the main entrance to Stockholm's world-famous open-air museum, Skansen Park, which attracts some two million visitors a year. Old log cabin farmsteads from various ages and differing latitudes between Lapland and Gotland have been brought here and rebuilt. Shielings, ancient craft workshops, Finn settlements, windmills, belfries, maypoles, smithies, sheepcotes, a beacon, and countless other rural relics of the past stand on Skansen Hill. Old country customs are revived—singing, folk-dancing in costume; and playing of old instruments is practised throughout the summer. Skansen is a cultural centre of considerable importance, a rendezvous for national conventions, jubilees and celebrations. As an open-air museum it is unique.

How strange that the water near the main entrance to this wonderful collection should now be yielding up a cultural relic that might well prove to be a greater attraction than any other part of the fabulous Skansen collection.

During 1960, when the raising of the galleon was regarded as an absolute certainty, the question of the siting of the Vasa Museum had to be decided. As considerable restoration work would have to be carried out after bringing her to the surface, it was decided not to place her in her final resting-place immediately. She would have to be mounted standing on a floating platform, while preliminary excavation and careful removal of the vast quantity of mud could be started. A temporary public exhibition place should be arranged where people could see her during the summer of her first appearance.

It was decided to set up a special Construction Committee, and Swedish consulting engineers gladly contributed their whole-hearted support. The Swedish
building materials industry offered to supply everything
needed—much of it at below actual cost price.

The committee's first consideration was given to the
permanent platform or floating pontoon on which the
Vasa would be placed during the early investigation by
the archaeologists and viewing by the general public.
This floating concrete pontoon was designed and built
through the joint contributions made by the consulting
engineers A.B. Vattenbyggnadsbyran and the four
contractors A.B. Armerad Betong, A.B. Akanska Cement-
gjuteriet, Nya Asfalt A.B. and Byggnadsaktiebolaget
Contractor, who formed the syndicate "Kvadraten".
The use of a floating dock was offered by the Gävle Dock
Company, and the pontoon, which measured sixty yards
long by twenty-three yards wide and twelve feet deep,
was made and launched from this dock on 21st April
1961. It was then towed from Gävle, a hundred miles
away, to the Gustav V Drydock, where it was sunk to
the bottom in readiness to receive its precious burden.

Work on the permanent Vasa Museum at the water's
edge, almost opposite the main entrance to Skansen
Park, was also started. Foundations were laid for the
workshops, lecture hall, observatory, exhibition rooms,
and a restaurant overlooking the water which was
intended to command one of the loveliest views of this
Scandinavian Venice.

Everyone concerned with each department of this
phase of the Vasa story in the spring of 1961 worked
extraordinarily hard. It was as though the spirits of the

The Vasa *mounted on her pontoon which now forms the floor of the house which has been built around her.*

A victim of the disaster.

One of the heavy cannon left by Von Treileben's men, discovered in the deep mud of the lower gun-deck, which became known as the dead man's deck.

Down in the orlop deck the two thousand barrels of food and stores had lain undisturbed for three hundred and thirty years, except for the gradual silting up of mud. Now at last the mud can be cleaned away and the contents of the unbroken barrels investigated.

Steel-helmeted archaeologists examining the morass of mud for the slightest particle of seventeenth-century remains. All the mud was carefully washed through sieves and here an ancient musket butt has been discovered.

One of the gun decks during the excavation. Lighting and pumping arrangements were quickly installed to begin the great clean-up. This picture shows white-helmeted archaeologists at work sorting finds among the broken gun carriages.

Archaeologists trying to adjust a broken gun carriage on the dead man's deck.

Shipshape once more. One of the firing decks when the mud had been removed and the gun carriages righted and restored to their positions at the gun-ports.

The Vasa 'stayed' upright on her great pontoon, with the pre-stressed concrete framework of the house in position. Slowly she makes her way from the dry dock to the Beckholmen Vasa shipyard where she was on exhibition during the summer of 1961.

During the autumn of 1961. The old ship gradually disappears behind a growing cocoon of tubular steel scaffolding as a prelude to the building of the aluminium house that will protect the Vasa *for the next decade.*

long-dead army of her builders had returned from 1627 to inspire their fellow citizens of the twentieth century to bring their proud ship back and show her to the world.

On the morning of 4th April the salvage fleet assembled at the naval dockyard and moved across the fjord to Kastellholmen inlet, where they had left the *Vasa* nineteen months before.

In addition to the Neptun Company's ships and pontoons, the naval submarine salvage ship *Belos* was also in attendance.

The two pontoons, *Oden* and *Frigg*, were now anchored wider apart, and between them lay a stretch of water of some fifty feet, wide enough to take the full width of the *Vasa*. The four rafts, which throughout the years of work on the project had remained anchored above her, were now grouped at one end to form a causeway between the two halves of the salvage fleet. Beyond the pontoons the salvage vessels *Sleipner*, *Belos* and others of the Neptun fleet were moored together with launches, tugs and a barge. This strange cluster of craft was bunched together some fifty yards off the rock islet of Kastellholmen crowned by its little castle.

Daily bulletins in the press and on the radio kept everyone in Sweden well informed of developments. Each day during the three weeks that followed the arrival of the little ships crowds of people passed along the causeway from Skeppsholmen to the rocky islet to stand and stare down at the mysterious patch of water that separated the two pontoons. Speculation was rife, and tension was mounting, for at that critical period no one could be sure of anything.

The key man of the project was the veteran salvage

chief, sixty-five-year-old, white-haired Captain Axel Hedberg, who after a colourful career with the Swedish Navy was on the point of retiring. Raising the *Vasa* was his last job, and for him those early days of April were tense and exacting in the extreme.

It was obvious that the last stage of the lift could not be accomplished with the two pontoons floating directly above the *Vasa*, as there would be no room for her to emerge between them. It was decided to keep them apart and raise the ship by means of hydraulic jacks mounted on the inside edges of the two pontoons. This entailed considerable modification in the plans for the final lift. Fourteen great hydraulic jacks were mounted on platforms which projected over the edges of *Oden* and *Frigg*. The original six-inch hawsers were changed for nine-inch hawsers, and the final stage drew slowly nearer.

Seven hundred invitations had been sent to people who had been concerned in some way with the course of events which had led up to that great day. These V.I.P.s were allowed onto the vessels for a close view of the raising operations. They included representatives of the hundreds of industrial organisations which had contributed so freely in materials and labour. There were journalists who had written about it, broadcasters who had talked about it, salvage crews, archaeologists, divers, civic dignitaries, leaders of the nation, Edvin Falting, and, of course, Anders Franzén, the amateur marine archaeologist who had started off the whole affair.

On Monday morning, 24th April 1961, crowds of Stockholmers gathered at vantage points about the

harbour to witness the *Vasa's* return. Kastellholmen was soon covered with people. Each boat of the salvage flotilla was dressed overall with bunting and the Swedish flags. Television cameras of Eurovision were primed and poised for the occasion. The pump crews stood at the ready beside the fourteen huge hydraulic jacks awaiting the order to start. Captain Axel Hedberg gave the signal, the power was turned on, the jacks began to work, and, slowly, the fourteen strands of nine-inch hawsers took the strain. Aircraft and helicopters circled overhead with film and press cameras at the ready, and all eyes watched the space of water that lay calm and unruffled in the spring sunlight between the pontoons *Oden* and *Frigg*. The *Vasa* film unit, which had recorded the project at every stage, had cameras on the deck, far down in the murky depths, and up above in a helicopter.

At three minutes past nine in the morning an upright piece of ancient black oak broke the surface of the water, then others appeared beside it, until two gently curving rows of near upright thick black posts stood out of the harbour water. These were the bulwark stanchions of the ancient wooden walls of the *Vasa*. Then, beneath the dim green surface of the water, the transverse cross-beams of the top deck began to show before they too broke the surface. Then the badly damaged upper-works of the ancient galleon once again emerged into the light of day. In the centre of the patch of water came the base of the foremast with its two carved wooden heads. The *Vasa's* return was greeted by a stirring fanfare from a group of naval trumpeters, and a burst of cheering welled over the water from the islands and the ships. It was a moving moment.

Then two figures stepped from one of the pontoons onto the blackened framework of the ship. One was Anders Franzén in his old white sailing jacket, the other was Edvin Falting in his diver's sweater. They were two men whose determination and courage have given to Sweden what posterity will judge to be its greatest national relic of antiquity.

The jacks continued to lift, and more of the damaged superstructure gradually came into view. Then very slowly the whole flotilla moved into shallower water.

On the following day Axel Hedberg decided to start pumping.

It was fortunate at this stage that the famous Flygt Pumps Company had offered the use of their mammoth submersible equipment, a Swedish invention designed to assist ships in distress. The big (B-200L) pumps had already been sunk into the *Vasa*, the power was switched on and the water was pumped out at the rate of two thousand three hundred gallons per minute. There were still many leaks and the water poured in at the rate of about one and a half thousand gallons per minute. But gradually the huge pumps prevailed and the *Vasa* rose higher and higher out of the water. It was not the first time that these powerful pumps had proved their effectiveness.

When the Japanese town of Nagoya was flooded in 1959, one and a half million people were affected and entire blocks of houses were destroyed. Among the calls for help which were sent out, was a cable to Stockholm for a Flygt submersible pump. The Scandinavian airline system took one from the Swedish factory. In spite of the fact that it weighed well over half a ton it was

flown over the North Pole by the shortest route to Japan, where it was put into action to reduce the extensive damage to property.

A cargo ship loaded with three thousand tons of ore was bound from Sweden to Germany when she ran aground and sank in shallow water. The salvage company lowered submersible pumps into the cargo holds, electrical power was available, and pumping was started. As the water level sank inside the ship, water poured in through the damaged hull; tarpaulins were used to cover up the leaks. Pumping was kept up day and night for three weeks and the ore carrier was gradually raised to the surface.

During the preparations for the opening of the great Saint Lawrence Seaway in 1959, five days before Queen Elizabeth and President Eisenhower were to arrive for the official opening, one of the great locks went out of order, all shipping was brought to a standstill, and panic seized the organisers. Nine Flygt pumps were rushed from Ontario and lowered into the water. The power was switched on, the channel was drained, and repairs were carried out. The inauguration of the great seaway took place on schedule.

Whether in Canada, Africa, Switzerland, Holland, Japan, Britain, U.S.A., Mexico or any other part of the world where trouble or disaster threatens, this remarkable invention plays its part. But no incident in the history of these pumps is more romantic than when they helped to keep the three-hundred-and-thirty-year-old wooden ship afloat in Stockholm harbour, and also kept her sprayed with water from bow to stern in April of 1961.

One by one the leaks were found by frogmen, who by virtue of their greater mobility in surface water were now replacing the conventional divers. For two weeks the great pumps kept working day and night and the frogmen continued finding and corking new leaks, until at last, on 4th May, Axel Hedberg judged that the *Vasa* was capable of floating unaided.

Vasa had to make the last hundred yards into the narrow dock floating on her own keel; there was no room for *Oden* and *Frigg*—not that she now needed them. Like a battle-scarred warrior who had learned to walk again and thrown away his crutches, *Vasa* left the two pontoons behind. Then the watchers were able to see the unique spectacle of an early seventeenth-century galleon afloat on her own keel in the port of Stockholm. Slowly, and with a slight list to port and a draught of twenty-two feet, she was hauled into the dock. The big salvage pumps still continued to work on the lower decks. The dock-gates were closed. The six-year long adventure of winning back the *Vasa* was over. Now quite different work could begin—the work of restoration and preservation.

CHAPTER 6

Inside the Galleon

THROUGHOUT the long period of underwater preparation for lifting, when the divers had bored under the ship and subsequently sealed up most of the leaks, no one had yet entered the hull. It was known that *Vasa* was a veritable floating museum of the early seventeenth century, and the interior was to be disturbed as little as possible until archaeologists could begin the task of careful excavation. The time for this had now arrived. Clad in rubber trousers, black oilskin mackintoshes and white steel helmets, they made their first exploration of the upper gun deck. The top deck had been completely ripped away by the early salvage of the cannon, and only the curved transverse beams remained. But the gun deck was firm below its deposit of mud.

The first and most urgent need was the prevention of quick drying of exposed timbers, which, if not treated, would quickly crack and open in the sunlight and air. Great quantities of plastic sheets were taken on board and the workmen began wrapping the beams and stanchions.

Then the dock was drained and the *Vasa* stood upright amidst a forest of wedged staying poles that kept her in position. The pumps which had worked day and night

to empty her were converted to work an extensive
sprinkler system which kept the woodwork sprayed with
water. Under such conditions the archaeologists worked
beside the scientists, labourers, electricians, carpenters
and employees of the Flygt Pumps Company. A few
privileged visitors were permitted on board, but *Vasa*
was not yet on exhibition. Entrance to the dock was
prohibited to sightseers, who might hamper the frantic
work to prepare her sodden timbers to withstand the
brightness of the Scandinavian sun. In the midst of
tons of slime and mud the work slowly continued.

Gustavus II Adolphus, who had ordered the building
of the ship, never set foot on board. It was left to his
distant successor, King Gustavus VII Adolphus, to board
her—which he did as one of Sweden's most distinguished
archaeologists. From the beginning he had been fascinated by the venture and had given the recovery programme his consistent support.

Sorting the valuable finds from the mass of filth was
enough to daunt the spirits of any specialist, but this was
the challenge of a lifetime and everyone worked with
inspiration.

Foot by foot the upper gun deck was cleared, every
item was washed, catalogued and sent to the museum,
and only after this was completed was access gained to
the lower gun deck.

This was the dead men's deck, and, illumined only
by the light from the cannon ports, it presented an
appalling spectacle of chaos and squalor. The depth of
mud on the slippery curving floor, together with the
low ceiling, made the archaeologists bend to avoid
hitting their heads in the gloomy darkness. It was at

The last journey of the Vasa. On a misty morning in November 1961, the Vasa, now completely housed, is towed at a speed of two knots from Beckholmen to the museum site.

The house and pontoon together weighed 3,900 tons.

The galleon seen from inside the house which was built around her in two months, an amazing operation.

The exhibition hall of the museum, showing the lion figurehead mounted at the proper angle at which it would appear on the Vasa's bow.

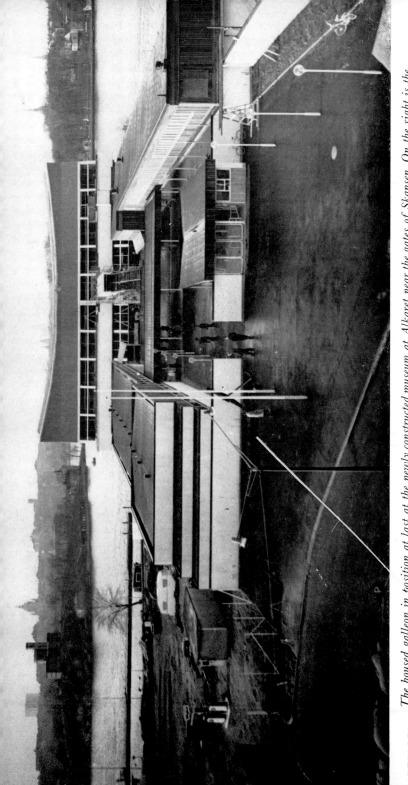

The housed galleon in position at last at the newly constructed museum at Alkaret near the gates of Skansen. On the right is the block that houses the administration offices, workshops and headquarters of the Vasa Board. On the left is the cinema lecture hall and exhibition room.

once an ordeal and the adventure of a lifetime for the steel-helmeted scholars, whose task was to sort out and miss no particle of interest or value in that fantastic jig-saw of history.

When the ship had originally heeled over and sunk, most of the armament had broken loose and crashed down the sloping deck to form a jumbled, tangled mass of gun carriages that were strewn along the port side. The whole scene, half buried in mud, was a sight that made a deep impression on the minds of these first investigators. The disclosure of a skeleton crushed beneath a two-ton cannon gave added poignancy to the disaster. Here were none of the splendid trappings of baroque art which had been retrieved from the mud in the early days, this was no gallery of marine architectural adornment, but the grim machinery of a fighting man-o'-war. There were long-handled ramrods, powder barrels, cannon-balls, pulley blocks, broken pails, copper powder shovels, and broken human bones beneath a tangled web of mud-covered ropes. This was the fighting end of the *Vasa*; for this reason was she dedicated to the glory of imperial Sweden.

When the electricians moved in and the scene was wired for lighting, the mud was carefully scrutinised before being washed away.

Finally, they penetrated down below the gun deck to the orlop deck, where spare canvas, ropes, kegs, boxes, fire-arms, gunpowder, tools, general spares and two thousand barrels of food for the maiden voyage were packed from deck to deck. The mud had largely preserved them. The weight in food and supplies is not known, but may be estimated at well over a hundred

tons. Below the orlop deck lay one hundred and twenty tons of ballast which consisted of round stones of between nine and twelve inches in diameter. These were removed by conveyor-belt.

While the Swedish archaeologists under the leader-ship of Per Lundstroem were laying their plans for sifting out the finds from the vast morass of mud on the various decks, others were planning the *Vasa's* next move on to her permanent pontoon. The water was allowed to run in and fill the dock. The old ship rose and floated to be drawn forward until her keel was directly over the keel blocks along the centre line of the pontoon. The water level in the dock was lowered and stay posts were wedged between the ship's side and the walls. Then the dock was emptied and extra staying posts were wedged in place until the gaunt old vessel resembled a rowing galley with triple rows of oars.

The pre-stressed concrete frames that were to carry the *Vasa* house were lifted one at a time by crane, lowered over the ship, and fixed to the pontoon. As this work went on, the scientists worked amidst the drip and spray of the water jets deep in the black bowels of the ship where they probed, sieved, and washed their finds. There was no time to spare, for the Board had promised that 17th June 1961 would be "Vasa Day" in Stockholm when the ship would be towed from the dock and taken to the temporary exhibition site nearby, where the public would be admitted to see her. This was the date for which the city waited. On 17th June the strangest contrap-tion that ever floated left Beckholm dock and was slowly towed across the harbour water.

If the statue of mighty Gustavus Adolphus, the

74

"Northern Hurricane", gazing fixedly towards the sea from his bronze horse in front of the Royal Opera House, could have recognised his lost ship standing on the surface of the water, arched over with concrete frames, he would surely have blinked his bronze eyes and gasped with wonder. The *Vasa* reached her temporary exhibition place nearer Skansen Park in a sheltered inlet which became known as the Vasa Dockyard. Here the public was admitted for the price of three kroner (about four shillings) to gaze at the great hulk, which, for seven years now, had been in and out of the city news.

At the Preservation Centre

LONG before the first sodden piece of timber appeared above the water experts were called in to apply the most modern methods of wood preservative to the steadily mounting haul of sculptures as they were brought up from the depths.

As the moisture in the waterlogged timber evaporated it was vital that its preservative properties were replaced. Experts in wood impregnation bored samples of oak from the interior of the timbers and conducted experiments to find the best substitute for the evaporated water.

A specially designed building was erected on the only piece of level ground on the already crowded rock island of Beckholm. It was a concrete structure about one hundred and fifty feet in length by about thirty feet in width. There were windows along one side, and offices, laboratories and workshops along the other side. An electrically operated movable gantry for conveying the heavier pieces hung from a rail which ran the full length of the ceiling. The gantry was built to lower the two-and-a-half-ton lion figurehead and heavy gun carriages in and out of the bath of preservative.

Chemical engineer Dr. Lars-Eric Barkman was in charge of the department.

Dr. Barkman's task was one of creative research in which he and his staff had to discover the best method of preserving the fragile discoveries. Small pieces of wood were removed from the interior of the timber and impregnated with glycol, linseed, acetone, chemical rust preventives and other substances.

The problem involved in these experiments was to discover a material soluble in water which could be impregnated deep into the fibre of the wood. On evaporation of the water, the solvent would be left within the cell structure of the timber. This process would reinforce the timber cells and minimise shrinkage and reduce the opening and cracking of the grain as the timbers dried out.

A method of wood preservation was developed by Mr. Tore Bostrom, a Stockholm engineer, by which impregnation with polyethylene glycol was carried out under vacuum-pressure. In order to prevent the timber from cracking, the wood was first steeped in a 30 per cent solution of polyethylene glycol, and after allowing the water to evaporate at a high temperature it was gradually replaced in the wood tissues by the chemical. In this way the shape of the carvings became stabilised.

This method was considered to be more effective for some of the finds. The sculptures while still wet were weighed, then the surface water was allowed to drain away. Then they were placed in a vacuum cylinder and the air was pumped away, the cylinder was then filled with polyethylene glycol, and the pressure gradually increased.

After the first impregnation, the sculptures were left

77

to dry out, the polyethylene glycol serving as a screen through which the water in the wood penetrated very slowly. When sufficient water had escaped, the vacuum impregnation process was repeated. When the moisture content had been reduced to normal it was found that the surface of the wood had regained its original form.

Excellent results were obtained by steeping the carvings in a heavily saturated solution of polyethylene glycol, and this method was finally decided upon for the woodwork. It proved to be the basic treatment employed throughout the entire preservation programme. Great quantities of glycol were brought to the centre, and the waxy material dissolved in heated water. Then one after another the figures of knights, mermaids, devils, cherubs, lions, dragons, reptiles, heraldry, and all the other precious finds were submitted to the heated concentrations in the tanks, until the water within them was entirely replaced by the solid waxy material.

In one place at the preservation centre a lady archaeologist was carefully working over the skeletal remains of one of the sailors. A zinc tray had been inserted under the remnants which, complete with the mud in which they rested, had been brought in for meticulous investigation. The leather shoes were still on the feet; traces of clothing were present in the mud. Part of the skull had been fractured, and it was presumed that the man had died violently. When investigation is complete, it is planned to bury the skeleton with all the other victims in the Stockholm Sailors' Graveyard.

Sections of the *Riksapplet*, another galleon contemporary with *Vasa*, had been raised and brought to the centre for controlled experiments. The galleon section

had been sawn into five pieces, and each piece was undergoing treatment with different forms of preservative.

During the search of *Vasa's* orlop deck (below the bottom gun deck) a spare sail had been found neatly stowed away. This too had been brought to the preservation centre and lay in one of the tanks of water outside the building. A piece of the sail fabric lay in a small container in the laboratory. Lars Barkman cut off a tiny piece and invited me to test its strength. It was remarkably tough. Then he put it on a glass slide beneath a low-power microscope and I looked through the lens. As the woven thread came into focus, protected and supported by its film of water, it seemed almost as perfect as it had been on the day of its weaving. The twisted threads of hemp were round in section, and every detail of the fibre appeared to be in good order.

Then I was given a remarkable demonstration to illustrate the preservative quality of water. Dr. Barkman took a warm-air blower and dried away the water on the slide, and even as the threads made contact with the air they began to collapse slowly like a dying plant when seen through a speeded-up film. The very substance of the hemp collapsed; it changed colour, from the natural tint of straw to a darkish brown; and as the air reached the inner strands, the pattern of the fibres disintegrated before my eyes. Three centuries of time were compressed into a period of as many minutes. Then the tattered particle of the *Vasa's* sail was resolved, like Rider Haggard's "She", into a grey amorphous ash.

In another part of the same laboratory a girl assistant was engaged in making moulded replicas of some of the

smaller wooden carvings. The idea of taking a mobile exhibition of the actual treasures to overseas countries could not be contemplated, for obvious reasons. So the preservation centre had been given the task of reproducing the carvings in suitable materials which could be used in travelling exhibitions. Experiments were being conducted with liquid plaster, warmed liquid wax, plastic, and other materials which were being poured into moulds and allowed to cool and set before the pliable moulds were removed.

I saw the glycol boiling tanks, and in them the gun carriages which were undergoing the glycol treatment. There were stacked tanks of water containing fabrics, ropes, copper articles, leather, felt, twine, and thousands of less-important wooden objects, all awaiting their turn at the hands of these white-coated experts, whose quiet patient work made the whole great *Vasa* venture.

As a child I remember reading and re-reading the haunting tale of a group of Siberian hunters who happened to be present when a mass of breaking ice suddenly revealed a perfectly preserved specimen of a mammoth. Feverishly they roped the mighty carcass up and staked it down for safety so that they could show it to their friends. But even as they watched in wonderment, the vast bulk of the monster began to shrink and disintegrate before their eyes. Like my tiny piece of *Vasa* sail beneath the microscope, it returned to the dust from which, by the laws of nature, it was several million years overdue.

Few visitors are allowed to invade the privacy of the Beckholm preservation centre. But on the afternoon of

my visit a museum curator from the Peabody Institute of U.S.A. was also present, and we were able to share each other's amazement at what we saw: the chests of little drawers where *Vasa* coinage and pottery were carefully catalogued for easy reference; the workshops, with high-precision lathe tools for making the specialised scientific instruments required in this work; the heater; the giant separator; the sprinkler system; and the atmosphere of quiet scholarly research that did nothing to conceal the spirit of dedication to the job that characterised Lars Barkman and his staff.

Then we were invited into the canteen for coffee and cakes and we talked of timber and ships and the old wooden walls of England and America.

CHAPTER 8

My Return to Stockholm

ON Easter Monday, 23rd April 1962, I returned to Stockholm and boarded the Skansen ferry-boat at Skeppsbron. Rounding the island of Kastellholmen, I was immediately struck by the fantastic size of the *Vasa* house. Standing out from the Skansen waterfront, its grey-green sides swept upwards in lines that followed (to some extent) the lines of the floating galleon.

On one side of it lay a miniature motor-boat harbour and the noisy panoply of the Tivoli fairground with its modern equivalent of roundabouts and swings. On the other side lay the naval dockyard with cranes, corvettes and submarines. Beyond this rose the towering spires of the Nordic Museum. The woodlands of Skansen Hill rose in the background, with its ancient timbered houses peeping from the greening trees.

I stepped ashore and walked over to the museum, which had been under construction on my previous visit. How would I react towards the Swedish presentation of the ancient ship housed as a museum exhibit, shorn perhaps of its thrilling romance of discovery and early excitement?

In Stockholm this present home of the *Vasa* is not regarded as a museum but merely another temporary home, where the huge hull will undergo the long-drawn process of preservation and where the carvings,

fittings and armament will gradually be restored to their original positions. It is anticipated that this exhibition site will exist in its present form until about 1970, by which time more final plans will have been made for the way in which *Vasa* will be bequeathed to posterity.

Beyond the turnstiles lay an open courtyard, with offices on one side, and a display hall, cinema and cafeteria on the other side. At the far end of the courtyard wooden steps led up to a covered gangway that gave access to the vast floating hall which contained the galleon. First I entered the large exhibition room where three hundred exhibits out of the twenty thousand finds were on show. But great care had been taken to display these representative pieces to tell the story of the original building and launching, the sinking, finding and raising of the *Vasa*.

In the centre of the floor, in pride of place, the two-and-a-half-ton lion figurehead reared up at its proper angle, as intended at the *Vasa's* bow. A cannon resting on a temporary wooden gun carriage stood nearby.

One wall was composed almost entirely of glass, and a row of display cases contained many of the smaller objects. There were metal boxes, pewter tankards and plates, a brandy barrel, earthenware pots, a broad-brimmed hat (perfectly restored), shoes, gloves, a tool case with a plane, drill, awls, plumb-bobs, and wooden handles. There were bronze coins dating from 1624, but the majority were minted in 1627. The silver coins were mainly from the previous century.

There were wooden pulley blocks, powder horns, musket-shot moulds, and numerous carved figurines.

On the opposite long wall carefully selected wooden statuary and ornaments were arranged, and on panels

between these groups the whole *Vasa* history was cleverly revealed.

Enlarged reproductions of the drawings from Francesco Negri's book on Treileben's early diving were shown.

There were also maps of the harbour showing the short but eventful movements of the ship in 1628 and 1961.

Little *Teredo navalis* was not forgotten: a piece of timber showing shipworm attack was displayed, with a specimen of the boring worm preserved in a jar of formalin beside it.

Franzén's core sampler hung in a prominent place, and below it, hermetically sealed within a double Perspex case, was the first tiny piece of black oak, no bigger than a finger-nail, the very beginning of it all.

Along the short wall seven glass-fronted tanks full of water were arranged, each containing a carved life-size wooden figure of a child musician in the act of playing an instrument: a viola, lute, psalter, bagpipe, violin and flute. The central figure had no instrument; it was the devil, with hands clapped over his ears, apparently unable to stand the sound of the celestial music of the cherubs. Unfortunately these seven figures had been carved in softer wood than most of the sculptures, and they had had less protection from the mud. But even though they had deteriorated they were clearly carved by the same hand, the hand of an artist far superior to the men who carved the vigorous work on the zoomorphic caricatures of beasts and men. These angelic cherubs had a subtle beauty which to me transcended anything else in the great collection.

As I stood looking at these fading masterpieces of art, I heard strangely subdued music coming from a concealed recorder. It was a haunting combination of

sounds from the kind of instruments which the cherubs held, slightly off key in the manner of the period, but with a dream-like melancholy which I found slightly disturbing. This was a splendid example of the genius of Scandinavian museum display at its best. Although I listened to that sad music of the drowned cherubs many times during the ensuing days I never grew tired of it, of such is the kingdom of real art.

Adjoining the exhibition hall was the cinema, where at two-hourly intervals between 11 a.m. and 5 p.m. the thirty-minute film of the raising, made by the Vasa Amateur Film Unit, was shown four times each day to some two hundred and fifty people.

After watching the film I was ready to climb the rough wooden steps and walk along the covered causeway leading to the great floating hall which contained the hull of the *Vasa*. The woodwork of the passage-way had been left rough and darkly stained in order to prepare visitors for what lay ahead. My excitement mounted as I passed through the glass doors on to the lower gallery, to lean on the rails and look up at the ancient "wooden walls of Sweden". My first impression was dominated by the aromatic smell of sodden oak, mingled with the faint whiff of harbour mud and the cool spindrift of fine spray that hissed from jets along the centre of the roof to spread over the timbers of the ship and keep them wet. The jets hissed ceaselessly while somewhere in the background the rhythmic throbbing of a compressor maintained the water pressure in the many sprinkler tubes fixed around the sloping walls. This will be kept up probably for the next ten years.

To see again this fantastic wooden broadside towering

above me was an exciting experience. I moved slowly along the lower gallery peeping in through the gun-ports at the lighted interior. I saw the great circular hole three feet in diameter where the base of the mainmast had been stepped and the main hatchway leading to the orlop deck below. Through another gun-port nearer the stern I saw the hollowed upright alder trunk through which bilge water had been pumped away in 1628, the bark still perfect. I moved on to the stern, from which all traces of the outer covering had gone. Taffrail, quarter-pieces, low counters, wing and deck transoms, cove gallery, balustrades and windows were missing, torn away at various times during the three hundred years of entombment. Most of these pieces had been retrieved and now lay submerged in tanks at the preservation centre, and will be gradually restored to their original places. What I saw were the plain foundation timbers. One of the bronze braces into which the pintles of the rudder had fitted was still fixed to the base of the stern-post. Above the lower gun deck level all traces of the stern had gone. I looked through the opening along the curving deck, now scoured of its mud and secrets; a workman was spraying the wood-work with an anti-fungicide solution. I mounted the steps to the upper gallery to look down on the curving lines of the long narrow ship, the upright timbers projecting from the sides like two curving rows of heavy fence posts. From this height it was possible to see how the ship had been built and to have some idea of the great strength of her construction. Everyone knows the strength of laminated wood of half an inch thickness where the grain of the middle layer runs at right angles to the grain of the

two outer layers. The wooden walls of *Vasa* were constructed on this principle, but the three layers of oak were some eighteen inches in thickness. The top-deck planking had gone, and only the cambered deck beams remained.

I continued slowly along the upper gallery until I reached the end, which gave a splendid view of the bluff bow where the bowsprit had once projected above the lion figurehead.

I moved on down the steps to the lower gallery again to look up at the bow where, on either side, the two round hawse holes (through which the anchor cables passed) looked blankly out from the rounded walls of the bow. Through the holes I could see the cable bitts, two enormously heavy pieces of timber fixed upright on the deck, on which the cables would be wrapped when riding at anchor.

This forepart of the ship, like the stern, had suffered badly from the anchors of three centuries of shipping and had now been reduced to basic fundamentals of construction. It was now shorn of the bowsprit, figurehead, gun-port lids, headrail, forefoot, headpiece, lace-piece and all the other colourful splendours that once embellished it. But in some way I found this bare skeleton of the bow more fascinating than I might have done had all the trappings been in place. So many of these things may seem unnecessary, but in reality they serve a vital purpose and contribute to the glorious design of these old-time timbered argosies of the sea.

The bow seemed to hold the attention of visitors even longer than the stern had done. I heard exclamations in many languages, some of which I failed to recognise; but one thing was certain: that surprise, wonder, fascination and awe were expressed in every voice.

I returned on several occasions to Vasa-Varvet to talk to the staff, to again watch the film, to ramble round the galleries, to look down on the ship and peep through the gun-ports, or watch the rapt attention on the faces of groups and parties of visitors as they listened to the story of the ship from the Swedish guides.

If the organisers thought that when the old ship had reached dry dock the first stage in the *Vasa* story was over, they might well regard the setting up of this fabulous museum as the second stage. The third stage must be the slow and careful preservation of the hull. It will pose very different problems from those set up by the wooden sculptures which could so conveniently be lowered unto tanks of heated glycol. Years will pass before the great hull can be allowed to dry out. Gradually the pressure in the spray jets will be reduced; between seven and ten years is the estimated time before the jets will be finally turned off. Until then, day and night, winter and summer, the pumping will be continued.

Piece by piece the carvings will be restored to their places on the decks, about the hull, and on the bow and stern, until eventually the *Vasa* will be partly returned—I repeat, only partly returned—to her former glory. But to achieve this goal the archaeologists of Stockholm must fit the twenty thousand bits and pieces of the *Vasa* fabric back into their original places. They rightly regard their task as the greatest jig-saw puzzle of modern times.

But the day will come when these dedicated specialists finish their work. Truly they will have brought back from the seventeenth century a hunk of splendour to add to the wonders of this modern world.

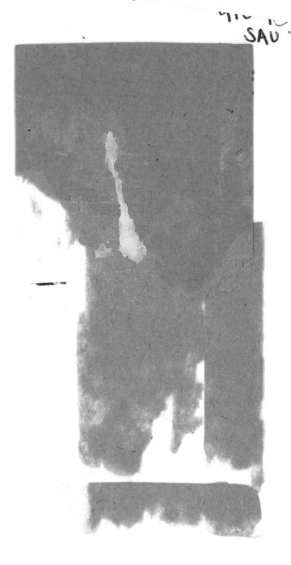